"This book has a nice display of opposing characters that all of us can instantly identify with, as I am sure we would have connected with these personalities at some stage of our lives. It certainly gives a different dimension on how we can deal with the everyday issues that we face in today's fast-paced world and lists the remedial steps that we can adopt to make it somewhat more amenable. Definitely a must-read for anyone striving to succeed and make an impact in this world."

— **Mok Yuen Lok**
Entrepreneur and Regional Executive Director,
Asia Pacific Crowe Horwath International;
co-founder and partner of Crowe Horwath Malaysia

"As a former CEO and current entrepreneur, this book resonated with me at the deepest level. The author's ability to understand the frustrations of modern life combined with his persuasive guidelines in our search for tranquillity and purpose makes for a compelling story — one which addresses the fundamental rather than superficial things that matter in our lives."

— **Steve Feniger**
CEO, 55 Consulting Ltd.; author of *Make It in China*

"This book takes us on a journey to find ourselves, inner happiness, and the true meaning to life in a time when we are constantly seeking material success. The story highlights the importance of cleansing our negative emotions. Only then can we have clarity for ourselves and be able to do good for others. What's behind you and what's in front of you is nothing compared to the power inside you."

— **Teh Lip Kim**
   CEO, Selangor Dredging Bhd

"An easy-to-read book that flows well with the characters. Not heavy reading; yet one would not dismiss it as light either, especially upon reflection on some of the stories, approaches, and sayings. There are many diverse parallels to life's experiences, beliefs, and paths. Keep an open mind and there is a lot to learn, understand, and appreciate from this reading. Definitely a push to introspection, or going deeper if one has already started."

— **Yong Yun Seong**
   Senior Director, Expedia Inc.; twenty-year Executive in multinational companies, including Microsoft, across different functions and industries

"I learnt a lot and really admire how you have managed to explain the teachings of Buddhism in a natural way, integrating very well in the worldly life. Really love the idea of the book, and I believe, the world needs a book like this. It can be both spiritual, as well as very practical for someone who wants to start making real changes in life!"

— **Agnija Kazusa**
   Mindfulness and Meditation Trainer; Manager at World Peace Initiative Foundation and Peace Revolution Project; author of two novels, *Bruno* and *Three Cups of Egypt*

"This is an inspired book, written very much from the perspective of a real practitioner and as such, filled with first-hand observations that are so relevant to our everyday lives. I am sure the reader will recognise much of him- or herself in the personalities of the protagonists. I certainly did; perhaps not so much in any one individual, but in the fears, emotions, and thoughts they all had. I recognised the paths they took as being very familiar, as being so human. So read this book, find out more about yourself, and most importantly, learn how to see things more clearly."

— **Low Huoi Seong**
   CEO and co-founder of Vision New Media content group and Vision Animation

A CEO
an Entrepreneur
a Tourist,
and the Monk

Finding the balance between success and happiness

ALEX BUTT

Candid Creation Publishing

First published April 2018

Candid Creation Publishing books are available through most major bookstores in Singapore. For bulk order of our books at special quantity discounts, please email us at enquiry@candidcreation.com.

A CEO, AN ENTREPRENEUR, A TOURIST, AND THE MONK
Finding the balance between success and happiness

Author	: Alex Butt
Publisher	: Phoon Kok Hwa
Editor	: Patricia Ng
Cover Designer	: Quek Hong Shin
Layout	: Corrine Teng
Published by	: Candid Creation Publishing LLP
	167 Jalan Bukit Merah
	#05-12 Connection One Tower 4
	Singapore 150167
Tel/Fax	: (65) 6273 7623
Website	: www.candidcreation.com
Facebook	: www.facebook.com/CandidCreationPublishing
Email	: enquiry@candidcreation.com
ISBN	: 978-981-11-6508-5

National Library Board, Singapore Cataloguing in Publication Data

Name(s): Butt, Alex, 1961-
Title: A CEO, an entrepreneur, a tourist, and the monk / Alex Butt.
Description: Singapore : Candid Creation Publishing, 2018.
Identifier(s): OCN 1028013080 | ISBN 978-981-11-6508-5 (paperback)
Subject(s): LCSH: Happiness. | Happiness--Religious aspects--Buddhism. | Success. | Success--Religious aspects--Buddhism.
Classification: DDC 158.1--dc23

CONTENTS

FOREWORD

Why have success and happiness been possible for some people but seem to have eluded others? What is true happiness? What is the meaning of life? Like many people, these questions have always been on Alex's mind. He spent twenty-five years in the corporate world and left that promising life to be an entrepreneur. He built a successful US-brand franchise and a consulting company focusing on helping companies grow leaders and teams. He is also a professional coach, training CEOs and international corporations around the world. After the unbearable loss of his beloved mother, he began to search for the real meaning of life besides thriving on business sphere.

Alex was ordained as a Buddhist monk when he joined the International Dhammadayada Ordination Program or IDOP (an intensive monastic and meditation training program for foreigners) in Thailand. This book draws directly from his corporate background and incorporates his profound understanding of the Buddha's teachings and lessons learned from living a simple life as a monk. Combining his CEO experiences with wisdom gained from the training, his view of life drastically changed as he realised the power of meditation and the true nature of the human mind.

Though there is no magic wand to alter life's suffering or problems into 'right-away happiness', this book will provide you with valuable concepts and the practical means to transform yourself to be successful and happy, no matter who you are and what you are pursuing. You will gain inestimable insights that will help you to build a habit of success and set unlimited worthwhile and measurable life's goals.

In my more than ten years of being a monk, this is one of the most 'painless to read' books I have ever experienced, with a clear chronological written structure and vivid explanations of the Buddha's teachings which everyone can easily relate to.

I truly believe that this book will help all readers who are in search of success and happiness find their way to enjoy living lives powerfully, passionately, and purposefully.

Phra Narongchai Thanajayo
Chief, International Dhammadayada Ordination and
Training Program

PREFACE

I wrote this book to take you on a journey by looking through the lenses of a CEO, an entrepreneur, and a Monk. The successes or failures of CEOs and entrepreneurs have been told in a lot of literature, yet, their inner thoughts, worries, temptations, and insecurities remain privy only to those who have lived it. Most of us were just normal people working hard to attain success and happiness, occasionally craving for only a thin sliver of Steve Jobs's creativity, Bill Gates's wealth, Jack Welch's leadership style, or the Dalai Lama's wisdom. Some people have aspired to be CEOs and to be their own boss as entrepreneurs, yet wanted to have the pure mind and kind heart of a spiritual mentor. Is that possible? Of course! But how? That's what this book will uncover for you.

WHO IT IS FOR

This book is written for those who are searching for the fine balance between material Success and inner Happiness. Are you the trailblazing executive? Adventurous gunslinging entrepreneur? Dreamy-eyed traveller? Or just stressed out, overworked, and wondering 'What the heck am I doing this for?'

WHAT IS IN THIS BOOK

This book contains stories inspired by the lives of CEOs, entrepreneurs, and friends whom I have had the privilege to meet, interview, coach, and work with over the last thirty years as a business person. In researching for spiritual inspiration, I had met monks who were Abbots, Teachers, and Mentors — from a personal perspective of being a student, a writer, a friend, and a neophyte monk. This book also contains interpretations of stories from my personal journeys to Thailand interacting with Dhammakaya Monks, and to Taipei's largest Mahayana Buddhist temple; and from the personal stories of a friend's twenty-five-year journey transforming from a Mahayana monk to attaining a PhD in Theravada Buddhism from Sri Lanka.

In our search for happiness, most people cannot escape the three poisons that defile our minds or souls. They are Greed, Anger, and Ignorance. In this book, the characters are not immune to these defilements despite their achievements of financial success, freedom, and inner peace. I have mixed the discourse of some of these teachings from a monk into a conversational format of questions and answers. I hope that this will provide an easier way to learn these topics, which are often written in large volumes of thick books interspersed with ancient words used to preserve their authenticity, but making them hard to read. In this book I have covered conversations on several topics: Ego and Self in Chapter 3; Meditation, Love, Compassion, Joy, and Equanimity in Chapter 4; Anger in Chapter 5; the Mind/Soul in Chapter 6; and Karma in Chapters 8 and 9.

The scholars of Buddhism will find that this book does not offer the depth and purity of Buddhist teachings. For me — and possibly many everyday seekers out there — I found learning Buddhism from reading books a difficult process. Not everyone can live socially connected, think like a monk, dedicate time to studying the Dhamma, practise meditation five times a day, and manage a successful business. This was one of the reasons I wrote this book — to introduce the key concepts from the teachings of Buddha and how I found the balance creating success, contentment, and achieving inner happiness at the same time. One has to read, practise, read, practise, read, etc... continuously in order to acquire wisdom. Wisdom will come when we practise these principles. When we meditate, the clarity of mind will lead us to a higher wisdom. It has been said; 'Knowledge is knowing; wisdom is acting on the knowledge at the appropriate moment'.

In writing this book, I also wanted the reader to receive some practical 'how to' business methods. Hence, I have introduced a life-priority-setting exercise and a team-building methodology embedded into the story. In Chapter 6, you will find the Life Inventory exercise which uncovers an individual's life's priority, called the Triple Gems. In Chapter 8, the CEO shares a powerful methodology called The Results Pathway for driving high performance teams.

RELIGION

This is not a religious book and I did not intend for it to advocate alignment to any specific religious beliefs or practices. The character of the Buddhist monk, Matt, allowed me to introduce a dimension of spiritualism and philosophy, which is pivotal for the topic of happiness, temptations, contentment, sins, karma, and the moral behavioural foundation from Precepts and

Commandments. In the business world, these 'behavioural foundations' may show up as a company's Strategic Thrusts, Core Tenets, Focus Execution Pillars, or Core Values. In the broad topic of spiritualism, I am sure I might have stepped over into some sensitive areas where some readers' opinions or beliefs may differ. With utmost sincerity and humility, I apologise. Life is too short to debate on whose belief is right, as each person's belief is their reality. I merely seek to share my experiences through these characters and how they achieved the transformation in their lives by letting go of their beliefs and by emptying their cup first; a simple process, yet not easy to follow through on.

LANGUAGE

There are references to words in the Pāli language, an ancient language used by Buddha 2,560 years ago. Many ancient scriptures of Buddha were translated into Sanskrit, the classical ancient language of India which precedes the Pāli language. The spellings in Pāli may be less familiar to most compared to the Sanskrit equivalent. For example, Kamma in the Pāli language is Karma in Sanskrit; Dhamma (Pāli) is Dharma (Sanskrit); Sutta (Pāli) is Sutra (Sanskrit); and Nibbana (Pāli) is Nirvana (Sanskrit). Sometimes these spellings may be used interchangeably by the characters to represent their familiarity and exposure to them. I try to preserve the Pāli spelling in this book as an acknowledgement to the sources of my research from direct discourse with teaching monks and literature on Buddhist teachings.

DISCLAIMER AND COINCIDENCE

Legal disclaimer: 'This book is a work of fiction. Names, characters, businesses, places, events, locales, and incidents are either the products of the author's imagination or used in a fictitious manner. Any resemblance to actual persons, living or dead, or actual events is purely coincidental.'

Really? Coincidental? What if I don't believe in coincidences? Well, I know that the characters in this book are purely fictional, but I cannot guarantee that you won't find anyone who resembles some description of them, in parts or whole. I did not intend to embarrass or expose anyone specifically, but if you identified someone who resembles the descriptions or has been in a similar situation, you better let them read this book! It could be an old encounter from my previous incarnation, before this lifetime, through the countless cycles of rebirths. Some names of places and organisations in this book are real and exist today while some have been changed to maintain some anonymity. If you found places in the book familiar because you had visited them in person or in a dream, or just felt goosebumps reading about it, trust your gut feeling; it's probably a déjà vu moment, a place that you had visited in your previous life. Nothing in our life's encounter is a coincidence, that's provided you believe in the Law of Kamma. If there are legal claims — hopefully these won't happen — trying to explain the Law of Kamma (Chapter 8) in the courts of law in any jurisdiction would require an argument using Theoretical Rationality against Practical Rationality (Chapter 9), which I doubt would make rationale sense to any judge, unless I persuaded the judge to learn meditation first. Anyway, believe in whatever you want, they are just coincidences ... or are they?

Some references to organisations like the Dhammakaya Foundation, Peace Revolution, and others mentioned in this book are interpretations from my direct personal experiences and research. Some references may not represent the actual intention and purpose of these organisations. I declare that this book represents my personal views and opinions, and does not attempt to be official representations for or on behalf of these organisations.

OPEN YOUR MIND

I hope you will read with an open mind, without arguing for or against any religious differences. Allow yourself to travel on the journey of these characters, imagine yourself walking alongside them. You might see someone familiar on this journey too, as I have. I hope you will enjoy reading it as much as I have had living it.

Our encounters in this life are not coincidences.
The people who appear in our lives are
the result of our wishes and
Kammic actions from our previous existence.
Meeting them here is our Reunion with them.
So, make the best of this life, build good merits,
and perform good deeds.
Be generous, sympathetic, compassionate,
and share loving kindness to all.
Have the courage to make good positive wishes
for yourselves and for others, daily.
May you discover success on this journey,
find your Triple Gems to attain inner peace,
and experience the blissful joy of ... Happiness.

- Alex Butt -

1

AUTUMN IN PRAGUE

God has no religion.
- Mahatma Gandhi -

Kampa Park, Prague

August. If the seasons represented the personality types of a person, then Autumn would be the Introvert. With the ending of the extroverted personality of an exciting Summer, Autumn opened the inner reflective and introspective personality. Autumn in Prague unfolded the deeper meaning of life against the golden colours of the foliage. Just like Truffle's deep and musky flavour bring distinction to a dish, Autumn unfurled the magic that brought romance and meaning to a person's life. The fallen leaves at Kampa Park reminded one of the poignant moments as a child, kicking piles of dried leaves and running through the park, carefree and happy. The moderate cold air and the warmth from the sun kept the spirits high as one strolled through the cobblestone streets. Couples held hands, laughing joyously in a tête-à-tête at the sidewalk cafes. Tourists snapped pictures with their phone cameras. Tour guides held bright flags at the end of their umbrellas, trying to hold the tourists' attention with their memorised scripts. Buskers performed classical music on strings and horns, infusing romance and love into the atmosphere on the historic Charles Bridge.

THE MONK

Matt Somchai was a monk from Thailand. Since he was ordained ten years ago, he had taught meditation workshops extensively in Thailand to English-speaking international visitors at the monastery. This time, Monk Matt was invited to introduce the Dhammakaya meditation method to a Czech meditation group. This was one of his international trips outside of the monastery. Matt spoke Czech because his father, a Thai national, was assigned to the Thai Trade Centre in Prague when Matt was growing up. The trade centre was a department within the Royal Thai Embassy.

Monk Matt was supposed to meet a guide here at Kampa Park. He chose this place because, as a child, he used to visit his father at the Thai Embassy in Prague District 1. Kampa Park is just behind the embassy where he spent countless happy moments with his mum after school. This was his favourite place where he felt free to run around without the restriction of the embassy rules. Nearby was the 25-metre graffiti-covered structure called the Lennon Wall. It was supposed to be the most soughtafter attraction in the area, where people from all over the world honoured John Lennon, the murdered member of the Beatles who became an icon of peace in the 1960s and 1970s.

While waiting, Monk Matt decided to meditate under a big tree, a tree that used to be about his height when he was twelve years old. These days, Monk Matt travelled around the world with only a passport, his sling bag, and a bowl. After he arrived at the Václav Havel Airport Prague, Monk Matt was dropped off at Kampa Park where he would meet a person named Theresa who would be his guide. After a twenty-two-hour flight, even a monk's mind was not immune to the toll of jet lag. Fortunately, the fond memories of his childhood occupied Monk Matt's mind, which helped him to overcome the awareness of the time difference. His mother had passed away a year ago, and he thought of her a lot. As a monk, he learnt to rejoice for her peaceful transition to the hereafter, instead of being saddened by the loss of his mother. Monks also have emotions, desires, and feelings associated with past relationships. The difference was that monks trained their minds, every day and every minute, to dissociate from emotions, feelings, and attachment to material things. They did this by chanting sutras and meditating. Being a monk required continuous mental training and refinement of the Mind, which is also referred to as the Soul or the Spirit. To a Hindu or Buddhist monk, this Mind, Spirit, or Soul—whichever term was used—was essentially the same energy that exists beyond the physical human form, through countless cycles of rebirths.

It was almost noon and Monk Matt was preparing to have his lunch under the tree. As a monk could not buy food, they receive food as alms. Theresa had located Monk Matt easily, spotting the distinctive yellow robe against the grassy park ground from afar, and was heading towards him. She was riding a pink bicycle—with a wicker basket filled to its brim hanging from the front handlebar—and avoiding the joggers who shared the narrow path in the park. She was the guide who had been assigned to Monk Matt for the duration of his stay in Prague.

Theresa Vitova was born in Thailand. She moved to Prague as a teenager to help her mother in her restaurant. Now she worked as a tour guide. She would visit Thailand once a year to refresh herself spiritually at a Buddhist temple, the Wat Phra Dhammakaya. When she learnt that a Luang Phi (that is how Thai monks are referred to) named Venerable Matt Somchai would be going to Prague to start a meditation programme, she was delighted to volunteer her services. In Buddhism, performing merits is a way of life. By sharing and offering one's time, food, and other means of support to a monk is considered the purest form of charity.

Theresa kneeled to offer the food to Monk Matt, who then started to chant to bless her for the alms offering.

A CEO

The Worldwide Sales and Budget Meeting for M-Reality Corporation had an action-packed agenda. Charles decided to skip a two-hour business networking lunch to sneak out for walk on the Charles Bridge. He smiled to himself: *A bridge named after me, that's nice.*

Charles, a corporate executive, had been stuck in the boardroom of the Mandarin Oriental Hotel for two days. He thought: *Why do we come to a beautiful place and not see the city?* He needed a smoke. So he asked his assistant to pack him a bottle of wine and some sandwiches so that he could lunch at the nearby park by himself. A seemingly romantic idea but, in reality, it was just an escape from all the chatter and shoulder-rubbing with the senior executive ranks.

Charles's mind was preoccupied by the new corporate market expansion strategies, product directions, and the increased sales targets for the new fiscal year. Many of the managers were still wondering if they could achieve these new targets. Charles had no doubts about meeting the new targets, but it would require major changes in his organisation immediately. Some guys would have to buck up and the bottom 5 per cent of underperformers would have to be fired. *Sigh!* He did not like firing people especially as a few of them were long-time employees who had given their lives to building this region's success. But the times had changed and these same employees had been stagnating while the new generation employees were thinking creatively and working hard to find new clients and capture new markets. He thought: *It's all about growth and numbers these days. If we don't grow, we lose market share. And that reflects badly on Wall Street. All our stock options would be affected and that's our retirement money.*

Charles sucked deeply on his cigarette, looking into the distance while thinking of the millions of dollars in stocks that matured every twelve months. He could retire comfortably now but to forgo the other $1.2 million of potential value of stock options would be such a waste. He needed to keep his job, keep doing his stuff, and keep the 'game in play'. He constantly reminded himself: *Look forward. Don't regret what we cannot change in our past. I have built a momentum and I cannot slow down now. This is the moment to charge forward. When I have enough… financial independence. I will retire. Then Amy and I can sail into the sunset and enjoy our lives together.* But how much was enough for him? He did not want to answer that question.

Charles found a quiet spot with an empty bench at Kampa Park overlooking the river. As he settled down, his eyes scanned the park. It was a self-defence instinct that he developed from his constant travels to places that were less safe. Charles knew that there were always crooks around who prey on unwary tourists. His eyes stopped as it caught a glimpse of the bright orange robe of a bald-headed monk sitting under a large tree about 15 metres away from him. He also saw a lady on a bicycle approaching the monk with a basket. He watched with interest as she kneeled and bowed to the monk. Charles Takashi Watanabe is a Japanese who had lived in Asia most of his life where Buddhism is a common religion. He spent fifteen years after college working in Seattle and had acquired an American accent. Embedded within an Asian culture, he displayed the facade of a Western business mind. Yet, in the areas of religion, Charles was agnostic. He never knew the difference between the monks from Japan who practised Zen Buddhism, or the Thai monks who practised Theravada scripture, or the Tibetan monks who practised Vajrayana Buddhism and followed the lead of the Dalai Lama. For some unknown reason, Charles decided to take some of his food to share with the monk. He did not know what made him approach the monk that day; maybe he needed some blessing for the huge sales quota he had been allocated for next fiscal year. Nonetheless, the decision would change his life forever.

AN ENTREPRENEUR

Antonio is an entrepreneur and a self-made millionaire. That morning, he stumbled into Kampa Park by chance when he lost his way trying to find his hotel. That was his first day in Prague. He had come to meet five friends from YPO (formerly known as the Young Presidents' Organization) at one of their quarterly gatherings which they call Forum Meetings. The YPO Network and Forum Meetings had helped Antonio tremendously in the past ten years. It served as his personal board of directors. He used these occasions as a platform to bounce ideas and share challenges while exploring how other entrepreneurs dealt with their obstacles. Over the last ten years, Antonio had preempted so many flaws in his business plans, which could have failed at launch had it not been for the Forum Meetings. These private discussions even helped resolve personal and family difficulties just by them learning from each other's mistakes and insights.

Antonio followed the travel website's recommendation to visit the Charles Bridge, which was a beautiful bridge with sculptures and stone-carved statues of figures from biblical history. Antonio had gone to a Catholic school but grew up in a Christian family with a strong religious background. He went to church most Sundays, whenever his travel schedule allowed. He believed that God had gifted him with his creative talent, his intelligent brain, and a healthy body. *It is up to me to make the best of God's gift.* He believed that going to church and saying prayers were an important part of a Christian life, but one should not totally rely only on prayers to make wishes come true or offer prayers only when one desperately needed God. He used to think, *People who rely too much on faith to guide their lives are leaving things in God's hands.* Antonio liked to take charge and to take risks and to take control. He felt that a person had to work hard, to solve problems creatively, and to make things happen. Waiting for God to answer one's prayers and perform miracles is not being accountable for one's own destiny.

Today, Antonio saw many stores along the streets selling a cone-like pastry called trdlo. It had the sweet aroma of a cinnamon bun and looked like an ice cream cone. He did a quick Internet search on his phone and discovered that 'trdlo' was the name of the roller the pastry was made on. It originated in Central Europe and is also known as 'trdelnik' in other countries. As Antonio walked around, he was amazed. At every building corner, there was a trdlo store. Every store had a long line of people queuing for their trdlo. His entrepreneur instinct was aroused. Antonio joined the line and bought a trdlo with vanilla ice cream, topped with chocolate on one side and strawberries on the other. Licking his lips, he thought, *Wow! It's delicious!* He studied the pricing of each cone and its various add-on options. He estimated the length of the queues and realised that this could be the next fresh concept for a fast snack food franchise business in Asia. He could start it in Hong Kong, where he lived, then expand to Shenzhen, China. Next, he would introduce it to the major cities of Beijing and Shanghai. The youth at these China cities would soak up Western-concept fast food. He thought: *It's going to spark an inferno of success in China.* He bought a few more different flavours from different stores, to test as field research. Now he needed to get to a quiet place to jot down his ideas. As he started to head back to his hotel, he grabbed a stack of napkins, not just for the drips from his melting ice cream, but to sketch the business plan while the excitement was still fresh in his mind. He walked through the back lanes looking for the shortest path back, took a few turns around Mala Strana Square and, instead of reaching his hotel, he ended up in a green open area called Kampa Park. He thought, *Well, this is a good place to inspire my big idea for a new line or product call Prag-dough.* He instantly liked his own idea.

A TOURIST

Antonio was balancing three cones of trdlo in his hands when he saw an empty bench 20 metres ahead and made a beeline dash to his target. A young man, walking with his head down, emerged from a path from his blind spot, slammed into Antonio, almost dislodging his precious trdlo. "Excuse me! I am so sorry!" the young man apologised.

Antonio was flustered and annoyed, "Hey, watch out man! Be careful where you are walking. You could walk into the river ahead." Toby, the young man, replied with deep sigh, "Ya, not sure if my day could get any worse than what it is already."

Antonio paused to look at the young man in torn jeans, a sweater with a hood, carrying a backpack. He looked depressed. Feeling extra compassionate, Antonio asked, "Would sharing these trdlos with me help make you feel better?"

Toby looked up at Antonio for the first time, then glanced at the trdlos in his hands, He instinctively licked his lips and said, "Really? Yeah! I am famished! I lost my luggage at the airport, lost my wallet too, and don't have a place to stay, and it's only my first day in Prague. Thanks! I sure could do with some food."

Toby was penniless. Today was an unlucky day for him. In fact, he had been unlucky since he was young. Toby was born with a hole in his heart, and due to that condition, he could not play most sports in school. He did not enjoy studying and struggled through high school. He learnt dancing from his father, who was a national dance champion in the 1960s. Toby became a talented dancer, winning competitions internationally. But in his father's eyes, he was never good enough. He was in and out of the mental hospital for depression and alcoholism. One day his wife left him. His three kids followed their mother because Dad was drunk all the time. After six months of rehabilitation at the mental hospital, Toby sobered up. He took all his savings, booked a ticket, and decided to backpack and work odd jobs in Europe for a year.

That morning, he lost his luggage at the airport—someone took it by mistake. His wallet was picked when he was on the bus. Now he had nothing with him—no luggage, no identity card, no money, and he was hungry. Desperately, he walked mindlessly, which lead him to Kampa Park where he almost knocked over Antonio.

Antonio sat down on the bench. Toby was holding on to three of the field research samples of trdlo while Antonio was sketching frantically on his napkins, lifting his head to look at Toby's reaction as he gorged on the samples and bombarding him with questions about taste, colour, Gen-Y and Gen-X taste buds, and so forth. They were both so engrossed in their research that nothing else at the park interested them… until a sudden wave of bright orange passed in front of them. As if by some divine force, they both looked up as a strange bald-headed person wrapped in an orange robe passed in front of them. A monk was walking barefoot, slowly and lightly with his eyes half closed. He seemed so calm and peaceful. Antonio and Toby stared, frozen in bewilderment. Their eyes followed the monk's graceful path as he walked towards a large tree. They then saw a woman with long silky hair, dressed in a turtleneck sweater, on a bicycle, riding towards the monk. Time seemed to stand still as Toby and Antonio continued to gaze at the scene where the monk moved, against the green background of the park, amidst people of all ethnicities and races in Prague. Antonio found this intriguing, as people may not realise that Prague was the centre of a religious conflict in 1620 during the Battle of White Mountain. Since then, the Czech people have tolerated the various religions that existed but for the most part, were indifferent to their beliefs. Despite all the manifestation of churches and biblical figures and statues on the buildings walls, the Czech Republic has one of the oldest least religious populations in the world. To see a Buddhist monk walking in a public park was a unique sight which put Antonio into state of suspended animation.

Toby looked at Antonio and reacted instinctively, "Finished? Let's go get some blessing from the monk. We could offer the last trdlo to the monk and maybe learn some kung fu too. Your business plan would be more successful when blessed by a monk."

Antonio questioned incredulously, "A monk in Prague? Could it be a scam? I've seen a lot of these monks while travelling in Asia. They begged for money to buy personal comforts. Some sell lucky numbers for lotteries… and..."

But Toby was already three steps ahead, grabbing some of Antonio's precious napkins on which he sketched his future trdlo carts and booth concepts. Toby used a napkin to wipe his sticky fingers and realised that he almost wiped his face with page four of Antonio's master plan.

FIRST MEETING

Monk Matt was settling down as he noticed several people approaching from different directions. A gentleman in a navy blue business suit and yellow tie holding a bottle of wine in one hand and a small basket in the other. A young man with a headful of curly hair wearing a hooded sweat shirt with 'Pink Floyd' printed across the front. A bearded man in a brown leather jacket scrambling behind the young man, heading his way with an ice cream cone in one hand and a bunch of napkins in the other, a pen in his mouth, and a knapsack on his right shoulder.

Monk Matt decided to wait for the men to approach before he started his lunch. Theresa laid three small mats on the grass for the visitors. She sat on another mat in a cross-legged position. Then she turned to the man who arrived first and asked him what he would like to do. Charles looked lost but asked if the Monk would like some wine or a sandwich. Immediately he apologised for offering a ham and cheese sandwich, thinking that it was inappropriate to offer meat to monks as he assumed all of them were vegetarian. But Theresa explained, "Theravada monks from Thailand, Sri Lanka, and some parts of South East Asia accept vegetable and meat as alms. They do not request or specify the types of food to be offered to them because of a traditional practice passed down from Buddha. There are monks from the Mahayana Buddhist sect, mainly from Taiwan and China, where the scripture of 'No harming of living things' has been interpreted into a practice of vegetarianism. Theravada monks are not strict vegetarians because of the alms practice, but they are responsible for maintaining a healthy diet. So you could stay to meditate or offer food to Monk Matt but it is advisable not to offer food with raw meat like sashimi, sushi, oysters, raw steak, or food with alcohol content. The monastic precepts do not permit them to consume intoxicants like alcohol."

Charles offered a packet of potatoes chips to the Monk instead.

Antonio and Toby arrived in time to hear the last statement about meditation from Theresa. Antonio was instantly intrigued. The three men looked at each other and nodded a quick acknowledgement of each other's presence. The Monk calmly looked at all of them, maintaining a slight smile on his face. When the three of them were settled in their seats, the Monk spoke in perfect English, "Hello, my name is Matt. You may call me Monk or Monk Matt. In Thailand, it's common to greet monks as Luang Phi. Elderly monks are called Luang Ta. I am here to conduct a ten-day meditation workshop for a group in Prague. They call themselves Peace Revolution Agents. Blessings to all of you for the chance to join us for lunch. What brings you all here?"

Charles, taking the lead, replied. "Hi everyone, my name is Charles Takashi Watanabe. You can call me Charles." He looked around making sure he got everyone's attention, just like a good presenter should.

"I am here for a worldwide sales leadership meeting. I have been stuck in the hotel Mandarin Oriental, not far from here, for two full days. I thought of taking a walk to see Prague, get a smoke, and some fresh air, before I leave tomorrow night." Realising the oxymoron of 'smoking' and 'fresh air', he stammered a little as he continued. "I was born in Tokyo, Japan, but I lived in Seattle, USA, for fifteen years. For the past three years, I have been based and live in Singapore, the regional headquarters for our operation. I work for M-Reality Software as the President for Asia."

Mandarin Oriental Hotel is a five-star hotel in District One of Prague. It is a prestigious hotel and Charles mentioned it, subconsciously showing his status and success. This was also part of his corporate training technique when delivering impactful speeches, by subtly mentioning key power facts and names.

Antonio nodded but was unimpressed by this corporate suit's ego-driven introduction. He added, "Hello, my name is Antonio Anger. I am an entrepreneur and businessman. I have been an entrepreneur since my college days. I came to Prague to refresh my mind, to find some inspiration, and also because I heard that it's a beautiful city. It's one of my bucket list places. Have you guys tried this trdlo stuff? It's amazing! If I could get hold of that recipe... I have written a business plan..." As Antonio scrambled to reveal his notes from the napkin, Theresa jumped in with a cheerful smile to deliver a well-scripted introduction.

"Hi ya-all!" She scanned the group, making eye contact with everyone deliberately, and smiled widely like a magician about to reveal a trick. Everyone smiled back, instantly attracted by her good looks. All except for the Monk who kept his eyes on the ground, avoiding eye contact with a female in close range, which is one of the monastic precepts.

"My name is Theresa. I am a private tour guide and a student at the Academy of Fine Arts in Prague. I've been engaged by a friend to assist the Venerable Matt Somchai while he is in Prague. I am half-Thai and half Czech. My mom was from Thailand and my father is a Czech from the military. I grew up in Thailand till I was twelve after which my mum brought me to Prague where I spent my teenage years. I studied graphic design in Paris and am currently pursuing a Masters degree in New Media and Art Conservation of Sculptures and Architecture. I work as a tour guide to pay for my school fees and expenses."

Theresa's bubbly personality and infectious smile kept everyone glued to her introduction. "I specialise in small groups and private tours in Prague. I speak four languages—English, Spanish, Thai, and Czech—and I am learning Mandarin because there are more Chinese tourists these days. So, that is a short introduction of me."

Toby felt the pressure was on him to say something. He was never comfortable with groups and social gatherings. He hated all these meetings as people tended to exaggerate their achievements and were insincere with their compliments. "Er... guess it's my turn right?" He looked around nervously, waiting for some sign to continue. Charles smiled encouragingly. He looked upon this young man like an intern in his company. As a CEO, he knew he needed to give his support to the younger generation and help develop their potential. Antonio was still arranging his napkins, wondering where page four went to. But he wanted to be supportive, especially to impress Theresa, so he said, "Go on Toby!"

Toby felt confident said, "Namaste!", thinking that this Indian greeting would be appropriate in the presence of a monk, not knowing that monks from Thailand do not use this manner of greeting. "My name is Toby Tanner from Malaysia. I am just a tourist in Prague. I just got out of the mental hospital where I was dealing with my depression. I am also an alcoholic. I am a professional dance teacher and I have, err, no, I had my own dance studio. I don't have it anymore—it's a long story. Everyone wanted me to do so many things, but all I wanted was to dance and compete. They told me I should open a dance studio. So I opened a studio. Then they told me I should expand my business. Everyone had ideas for me to do so many things. But I didn't really want to do it. I married my dance partner ten years ago. Eventually, even she got fed up with me because I only wanted to dance and compete. I didn't like to run a business or teach beginners. I don't mind teaching champions, but not beginner's dance classes. Sigh! So I started drinking and was drunk most of the time. Finally, my dad forced me to deal with my alcoholism because it was affecting his business. By then, my wife had had enough of my depression and alcoholism, so she left me. I spent my last dollar to get here because a friend told me that his brother in Prague might have a job for me. My luggage was lost at the airport and the airlines have not been able to trace it. And even if they do, I don't know how they are going to contact me because my mobile phone has no roaming plan." Toby sighed deeply, relieved that he finished his life story in one breath. Then he added the final punch line of bad luck, "And while coming here on a bus, someone picked my pocket. I don't have money or ID with me. Luckily, I have my passport as I put that in my breast pocket." He looked around for sympathy, shrugged and concluded, "That's me." He forced a smile to lift his negative spirit.

Antonio, Charles, and Theresa all looked sympathetically at Toby.

Monk looked at Toby with a look of serenity and compassion and said in a slow, calm voice, "Maybe someone from our local meditation group could help you sort out the police report for the loss of your wallet." Monk looked in Theresa's direction.

Theresa nodded, "Let me check if there is someone who can help you with that."

Monk Matt continued, "In the meantime, while we are all here, we still have to eat right? There is enough food for everyone if you would like to share. Theresa has brought a feast to feed the whole park."

Everyone was relieved that Monk Matt had a sense of humour. The three men shuffled their food around, shared the bottle of wine, and had a merry meal at the park sitting around the Monk under a shady tree. The rays of the afternoon sun shone through the gaps of the leaves and provided this group with some warmth amidst Prague's chilly autumn weather. There were lively exchanges of conversation. Theresa explained her private tour guide services to Charles, who had the intention of engaging her for the next day as he would have half a day before his flight. Charles, influenced by Antonio's infectious energy, was interested to invest in the latter's start-ups of technology businesses. Toby contributed his ideas on how to use technology to make things more efficient with phone apps and social media marketing. The Monk just ate his small portion of the food, observing attentively yet indifferently, to the interactions of his new small congregation at the park. He ate quietly, with his eyes looking mostly into his bowl, without spilling the food or licking his fingers. Even dining etiquette was spelt out in the monastic precepts for monks. Amongst them were eating without talking and treating food as elements to nourish the body rather than choosing food based on flavour, looks, appeal, or brand. When Monk Matt finished his food, he wiped and dried the bowl with tissue paper till it was squeaky clean; a practice taught in monk school. Then he looked up at this group who were obviously enjoying the wine, cheese, sandwiches, chips, brownies, and trdlo.

Charles noticed that the Monk had finished his food so he turned his attention toward Monk Matt to ask a question.

2

KUNG FU, MORTALITY, AND SEX

All I have seen teaches me to trust
the Creator for all I have not seen.

- Ralph Waldo Emerson -

WHAT MAKES A MONK?

"Excuse me... er... Monk Matt, is that how I address you?"

Monk Matt smiled, "Yes, that would do."

Charles then asked, "Monk Matt, what makes a monk a monk?"

Everyone looked at the Monk, wondering if he understood Charles's question because from the look of their faces, they did not get it. The Monk closed his eyes, as if searching for an answer.

Charles, sensing that he should clarify his question, continued, "I mean, what does a real monk do? Do you practise kung fu? Can you see the future or someone's past? Can you grant wishes? Or do you meditate and levitate? Sorry for my naïveté. I don't really know about these monk stuff."

Antonio joined in enthusiastically, "Yeah, I heard that monks can live for over three hundred years in the forest. And they can survive for days without food. Is that true?"

Toby said shyly, "Is it true that a monk cannot have sex? That he has to remain chaste for the rest of his life?"

Monk maintained a smile and waited for them to unload their questions. Then he said, "Great questions! Where do I start? How much time do you all have?"

Everybody looked at each other and shrugged, indicating they had as much time as was needed.

SEX

Monk turned first to Toby and smiled, "Yes, chastity is part of our precepts. All sensual desires, pain, and pleasure are associated with the six sense organs of the body. These sense organs create desires and pleasures that will lead to displeasure and suffering eventually. When we react to the stimulation from the six senses of Sight, Hearing, Smell, Taste, Touch, and Thought, our minds gets attracted and attached to these sensations. If the sensations are pleasurable, we desire more. For example, when we taste something pleasurable, like the trdlo, we want more of it and have an expectation of how it should taste. When we buy another one from another store but do not get the same crunchiness or cinnamon flavour, we could get disappointed and angry at being cheated. This is suffering. When we see a beautiful girl, we are attracted to her beauty. We keep thinking about her day and night. We may even start to look at our own girlfriend or wife with certain expectations to match our impression of this beautiful girl. This leads to suffering. Similarly, sound, smell, taste, and touch lead to the other desires. Sensual desires generate intense pleasures which affect one's mind. When one is in love or sexually aroused, one's mind loses its clarity, logic, and conventional direction. Hence, monks who practise meditation must learn to avoid all sense desires. I guess that's where the expressions 'love is blind', or 'out of their mind', or 'crazy in love' come from."

Toby looked depressed, "No sex! That's a bummer." Theresa sighed deeply as she recollected those uncomfortable situations when her clients made subtle sexual advances.

Charles looked far away, trying to grapple with this concept that sexual desires were bad. He did not want to accept Monk's logic, yet, he could not disagree that his own misguided senses had lead him into a secret extramarital affair with a co-worker years ago. Even though it was over, he was constantly haunted by this one act of infidelity and the feeling of stupidity, anger, shame, and guilt were not easy to get rid of.

Antonio just looked disinterested with this topic of relationship and sex as he had always been too busy for any romantic relationships. He felt that courtship took too much effort and was a waste of valuable time. People should be upfront and say whether they like each other or not. He, however, frowned at the monk's explanation that sensual desires led to suffering. He enjoyed the pleasure of great gourmet food, the exquisite taste of fine wine, and his love for extravagant living. He thought: *Nope, I think those who have not tasted the pleasures of good living don't know that this is enjoyment. It's not suffering — its heavenly!* He smiled to himself.

KUNG FU

Monk, sensing the discomfort in the group, turned to Charles and laughingly said, "About kung fu, you must have watched *Kung Fu Panda* or some old Shaolin monk movies."

Everyone nodded and sniggered. Monk lifted his palm in a gesture of a karate chop and smiled, "Sorry to disappoint you. No, I don't know kung fu. I am a Thai Buddhist monk, not a Shaolin Buddhist monk. There is a particular temple in southern China called the Shaolin Temple where monks practise martial arts as a form of discipline for the mind. In Thailand, monks practise meditation to discipline the mind."

Charles laughed loudly, "Yes, loved that *Kung Fu* drama television series in the 1970s. I love that Kwai Chang Caine character." Charles did a few kung fu moves with his hands.

Antonio added enthusiastically, "The best scene was when the Caine character had to pass the final test after an eighteen-chamber obstacle course. As he walked into the eighteenth and last chamber, having overcome all obstacles and masters from the previous seventeen chambers, he faced his final challenge. He had to carry a large brass pot filled with hot coals by clamping it between his forearms. The engravings of a dragon and a tiger at the sides of the pot were branded permanently on his forearms. So cool!"

Theresa's face contorted into a pained expression.

Charles straightened up, "I love the other scene when his blind master said, 'As quickly as you can, snatch the pebble from my hand. When you can take the pebble from my hand, it will be time for you to leave.'"

Charles picked up a few pebbles from the ground and stretched his hands out to Antonio. Antonio pretended to be the disciple and focused on the pebbles in Charles's palms. He readied his right hand to do a quick snatch. Then he looked up, over Charles's left shoulder and pointed his left finger with a surprised expression. Charles turned his head to look in the direction that Antonio was pointing. At that moment, Antonio snatched the pebbles from Charles's open palm with his right hand and shouted, "Yeay! I got them! I got them!" Charles turned back to realise that he had been tricked. A wave of fury started to rise, but he suddenly saw the humour of the situation and burst out laughing. Then, Charles said in a low voice, "Grasshopper, it's time for you to leave!" Antonio played along and bowed respectfully, then pretended to pick up his bag to leave. Both Charles and Antonio high-fived each other before laughing and clutching their stomachs.

Theresa and Toby looked lost. Theresa said, "Hey, don't show off your age. That show must so old that it's kept in the deepest archived section of some dusty film storage."

Monk was pleased to see these strangers getting along so well. He smiled and continued, "A monk lives a simple life. With simplicity, the mind gets clearer. Monks meditate to nurture a clear and bright mind. We do not grant wishes. Through meditation, some Indian yogis claim to be able to fly or levitate. If you want see a person fly, perhaps you could go to Las Vegas and watch David Copperfield's magic show. He did not have to go through being a monk to fly."

Everyone laughed.

Monk Matt continued, "For monks, we focus on meditation and obtain the power of a pure mind to gain inner wisdom and help others by spreading peace. Meditation is not restricted to monks. Even laypeople can practise and master meditation. It has been around even before Buddha's time. Buddha introduced forty different styles of meditation. Meditation will lead one to an inner power that the conscious mind can never achieve."

Antonio asked, "Power? Like seeing the future?"

Monk laughed, "Future? Hmm, do you want to know your future? What would knowing the future be useful for? Most people I've met want to know the future because of several reasons: financial gain, changing someone's behaviour, or avoiding death." He paused for a bit before continuing, "What is possible with meditation are an inner power beyond physical strength, as well as an inner wisdom to understand the truth of life, the law of the universe, and seeing our past lives. By attaining a state of mind that has no thought and is at complete standstill is the ultimate goal of advanced meditators. But seeing the future, hmm... it is better not get ahead of ourselves."

SIMPLICITY

Toby stammered, "What is a simple life? I want my life to be simple, but everyone expects me to be different. Other people make my life complicated."

Monk replied, "A baby cries when she is hungry. Once she has her fill of milk, she goes to sleep. Is that a simple life or an ignorant life? Life gets complicated when we grow up and start to acquire knowledge and accumulate material possessions. A simple life is... hmm... Ok, let me ask you all, how many things do each of you possess?"

Everyone looked puzzled.

Monk rephrased his question, "Do you know the total number of items that you possess, that you call your own? Pairs of shoes? Handbags? Cars, houses, suits, T-shirts, or anything that belongs to you?"

Theresa looked guilty, for she had lots of designer shoes and handbags.

Monk added, "How many pieces of clothing do you have in your wardrobe? One for every occasion, a set for different seasons, and different brands?"

Charles looked at his suit as he glided his hand over the cashmere wool fabric, enjoying the texture. He loved nice suits and his cotton shirts. He had different types of cotton for his white shirt collection. It filled one entire cupboard and he needed a separate one just for suit and pants. He loved his walk-in closet at home.

Antonio was thinking of his wristwatch collection. He loved his collection of Rolex, Ball, Omega, and Panerai watches, as well as his limited edition timepieces of various brands, totalling more than fifty pieces. They were all locked up in a custom-designed cabinet with a built-in watch winder to keep the semi-automatic watches wound all the time. Some days, he just sat in front of the glass display cabinet for hours, enjoying his timepieces with a glass of his favourite Chateau Trotanoy Pomerol and classical music playing in the background on his McIntosh, a handcrafted vacuum tube audiophile system.

Monk went on, "A monk's possession consists of only four items: two sets of robes, a bowl, shelter, and medicine. We don't own property, money, and other material assets. Of course, in the modern age, even monks need a few additional items to fit into society, like a cell phone and a laptop for teaching. But I don't own them, and I can do without them. We live in a small hut and sleep on a bed without a mattress. With fewer things, it is easier to maintain and clean. Monks don't waste time dealing with finding misplaced or lost items."

Theresa asked. "How about body creams, face washes, and shampoos?"

"We don't use creams to beautify our skin." answered Monk. "Creams or ointments for medicine are allowed, but not for embellishing our looks. That's why monks don't keep their hair as it would need care and combing. Monks don't eat after midday and that saves a few extra hours for meditation. By eating less, the body goes through a daily fasting process which helps to detoxify the system regularly."

"I understand that simplifying is practical for cleanliness and saving time. Is there a deeper spiritual purpose for simplicity?" asked Charles.

"Yes, there is." replied Monk. "When things are less complicated, they do not distract the mind. We can focus on meditating and performing good deeds. When one has few material needs, desires are reduced, and cravings are minimised. Craving, thirst, and desires are stimulated by our six senses — Sight, Hearing, Smell, Taste, Touch, and Thought. The sight of beautiful or disgusting things creates mental concepts of likes or dislikes and feelings of love or hate. Smells of fragrances from perfumes invoke sensual desires. The aroma and sight of food triggers desires for food regardless of hunger, which leads to extravagance. Speech and discussions influence the mind to create opinions, perceptions, and judgements. The mind generates thoughts, creates mental forms and feelings. It constructs complex attachments to things we agree, disagree, hate, or love and other complex human feelings. Hence, these six senses are the gates to greed and desires, which must be guarded against."

This prompted Toby to ask, "So monks are just emotionless and indifferent people? How can they not be affected by these senses at all? How can monks deal with the human emotions like on the death of loved ones? Monks are still human, are they not?"

Monk answered, "Yes, monks are also human, with feelings, desires, and temptations. For example, my mind is confused by the time zone difference when I travel. Sometimes, due to jet lag, I do not have the appetite to eat during lunchtime, so I will feel hungry in the evening when I am not supposed to eat. Monks use meditation and chanting to refocus the mind to avoid these desires and temptations."

"So monks would rather go to sleep hungry and bypass the biological need for food. I hate going to bed hungry," said Toby.

Monk explained, "I just drink a cup of green tea. Then I meditate and sleep it off. It works. Just like athletes who bypass the muscular fatigue and pains to keep going, we train the mind to overcome the biological and psychological sensors.

"In this society, unless you are secluded in a forest, most monks are surrounded by things of desire too. They still have family or friends and lay supporters who visit them. A monk trains his mind to consider these as impermanent assets that he does not possess, does not control, and is detached from. When monks lose a family member or a brother monk, they do not feel the suffering of the loss. They do not focus on the physical bodily aspect of the person — like their looks, their touch, their smell — nor do they think about the emotional friendship or love relationship of the person. Instead, they recollect all the good deeds of this person, rejoice in his merits and wish for his passage to heaven. When a bad situation improves, like when they suddenly receive a donation to support their peace mission, they rejoice in it, but they do not expect it to be a constant, hence avoiding the disappointment they might feel when the donation stops. That is the spiritual benefit of simplicity in a monk's life."

Charles quipped, "Simple things are not easy to do."

Toby was enlightened by the truth of this statement, and paraphrased aloud, "Yes indeed! Being simple does not mean it's easy to do these things. So true!"

Antonio scratched his head, "I've read about those Japanese Zen followers who practise a minimalistic lifestyle. One guy on YouTube showed how he reduced his possessions to only one hundred and fifty items! He claimed that a normal person probably owns over one thousand personal items. If the world goes in this direction of minimalism, then the consumer-driven retail economic model of supply and demand would collapse!" He sighed aloud.

Monk smiled, "Or a new economic model would evolve around this new dynamic. People's needs will change. This would influence the development of a new consumer economic model in this world. You have already seen new economic models that had disrupted the traditional business model. Online retail by Amazon has put some traditional bookstores out of business. Uber has transformed the public transportation industry where individuals can convert their personal cars into income generating tools. Airbnb has challenged the hospitality industry, Video and music streaming had replaced Tower Records and Blockbuster Video and other video and music rental businesses. Would you have imagined that very few people carry traveller's cheques anymore? In the future, e-wallets will pay for everything. The once popular credit card will be obsolete, like the traveller's cheques of yesterday. In fact, many students have cash cards and mobile payment apps, and these will eventually eliminate the need to have cash in their pockets. People can even borrow electronic cash using their mobile phones. People can even split a meal by using a mobile app to pay each other for their share. Who knows what else can evolve in our society?

This prompted Toby to ask, "What if everyone becomes a monk? Who will be fuelling the economy to support the monks and temples? Would there be no commerce?"

Monk gave a low chuckle, "It is very unlikely that everyone on earth would be a monk, at least not in this lifetime or a hundred lifetimes. There will always be people who are attracted by and destined to a life of simplicity and renunciation and who take delight in the spiritual teaching above all else. However, there are people who are attracted to success in the secular world while supporting and searching for their spiritual mission and purpose. And there will be some people who will oppose any form of structured and organised religion above all else.

"If the time comes when the majority of people are able to attain a spiritual level of enlightenment, then the level of spiritual consciousness will reach an advanced level. Universal love will prevail over mankind. The world will operate on a different currency. There will be no hatred, no war, no jealousy, no anger… just pure love and kindness. That will be the new currency of such an economy."

Charles, Antonio, and Toby looked at each other incredulously, not knowing how to accept this information. Charles was not in favour of such an economy as his stock options would be completely devalued. Antonio was trying to figure out if there might be an opportunity for early investment to monetise on the new currency. Toby's mind drifted as he pondered about Monk's words 'the level of spiritual consciousness will reach an advanced level. Universal love will prevail over mankind.'

Monk, sensing the mixed reactions, added, "You don't have to worry about that. Just focus on finding your own purpose and your mind."

EGO AND SELF

Turning to Antonio, Monk addressed his question, "About old monks who live in forests. I too have heard about a four-hundred-year-old monk who showed up at the temple every few years and disappeared back into the forest. No one knows where he came from or where he went. Personally, I have not met such monks. Maybe it's a myth, maybe it's real, I don't know. But in Thailand, there are many stories about these reclusive forest monks."

Antonio's mouth fell open, his eyes widened, and he gasped and murmured, loud enough for all to hear, "So it's true! Wow! If I could live that long… wow!" His mind started to imagine starting a business around an online meditation app. Using a subscription model, it could be the solution to anti-ageing stress, and living longer. *That would be a bestseller*, he thought as he scribbled his idea down.

Monk went on, "I have also heard that forest monks who meditated in seclusion did not need food. They'd reached a level of meditation which slowed down their metabolism and reduced any need for external sources of food to maintain the function of their organs. I have not seen or spoken to any monks like this even though I have been a monk for ten years and learnt meditation from various masters.

Once I joined an old monk who is a master meditator to meditate in a secluded temple for six months. We only had one meal a day. Once every fifteen days, we fasted for one day and meditated the whole day. We took a short break every three hours then meditated again. We did not need much sleep. We consumed less and less food. I lost fifteen kilos, but was healthier than ever. My master fasted for three days without food and water. He meditated the whole time. I could not do that, yet. But some day, I want to go back to just meditate full time and be free from a monk's daily duties at the temple."

By now, everyone was amazed by the possibility of meditation.

"Mr. Monk, I mean Matt, ahh… I mean Mr. Monk Matt… could you teach me how to meditate?" Antonio blurted what was on everyone's mind.

Monk smiled, "Just call me Monk Matt or Luang Phi, as the Thais would call us. As monks we practise Anatta, the concept of 'non-self'. So, any use of 'I' is regarded as identity and self. Thus, Monk Matt would refer to himself as Monk Matt, or Monk, or Luang Phi, so as to avoid using 'I'. By practising non-self, one removes ego and self-centredness. And yes, if you have time, Monk Matt would be glad to guide you on a short meditation afterwards."

Antonio nodded while reflecting on the ego and self-centeredness concept. *So true*, he thought, looking at Charles whose entire conversation 30 minutes ago was all about himself and boasting about how his organisation was the largest software company in the world. He said they were building the latest Augmented Reality — or AR, as it had come to be known — technology and claimed to consider licensing it to Google and Apple. Charles spoke about how this would change the consumers' experience in everything they do. For example, consumers could try a dress on before buying it, without ever going to the physical store; and online games could be played with people across nations on the phone and the games could integrate the users' own current environment, like a park. While all his talk was boastful and egocentric, Antonio found it inspiring. Antonio admired Charles's confidence and positivity. Yet, he struggled with how to fit a non-ego mindset into this material-driven world.

Theresa took the opportunity to add, "Monk Matt is here in Prague to conduct a Meditation Workshop at the invitation of a local interest group called Peace Revolution. We will be having a public meditation workshop tomorrow evening. If you are interested to attend, I can give you the website at which to register."

Charles, feeling uncomfortable with the ego and non-self concepts, sprang a question, more as a self-reflection than a directed query, "So, if we remove the 'I' and 'Ego', how do we market our products and compete as the best in the world and make customers happy?"

Antonio nodded vigorously because Charles just echoed the exact thought he had.

Pointing to Theresa's bicycle that was lying on its side next to her, Monk asked, "This object is what we call a bicycle. Once we disassemble it into its components, would the wheel or handlebar be called a bicycle? When we take it apart further, into tires, bolts, nuts, and frames, we start to describe them as individual components. The whole object has lost its identity as a bicycle. Ultimately, they are just metal parts, aluminum tubes, and rubbers. In the same way, a person's identity is a culmination of the various parts that form the body — cells, muscles, bones, organs, and so on — as well as his clothes, personality, hair, eyes, speech, etc. We are represented by all these components put together, creating the egocentric 'I', which gives us our sense of importance and significance. That forms the Ego.

"The parts of a bicycle have limited use by themselves. When combined into a bicycle, they become a transportation utility that can bring people conveniently from one place to another. But, compared to a motorcycle, a bicycle is slower, and compared to a car, a motorcycle is less comfortable. Similarly, our body parts are not very useful individually.

However, bring them together into a well-formed human body and they become a highly efficient system that can think, see, smell, hear, touch, taste, and do things. The individual person is less efficient than a well-managed organisation or less powerful then a well-trained army. Nonetheless, we use Ego to lift a person out of depression, raise self-confidence, or motivate to achieve greatness. Conversely, too much Ego can lead to over-confidence, arrogance, or tyranny. Thus, the disassociation of 'I', Self, or Ego is not to ignore its existence, but to acknowledge that it can help us get things done, think creatively, solve problems, and communicate. We need to balance it so that 'I' is not the only reason for everything, hence Egotism, in this sense, is the practice of the middle way towards the balance of success and happiness."

Monk, sensing the confusion, asked, "Would you like an example?" This elicited earnest nods from all of them.

"Let's say Charles created an enhanced software with new features that supports Apple's latest iPhone feature on Augmented Reality. Millions of people would get this as a free download. With this, they can transform any living room into a library, a war room, or any locale they want. It would improve the user experience and people would be able to have an enhanced experience using their smartphone devices with this new update. Would that be a good thing or a bad thing?"

Charles smiled, impressed by Monk's ability to use AR technology in his example. It changed his perception about monks being people who were escapists from the real world and that they could not fit in. He used to think that monks were society's dropouts, that they escaped from the society to seek reclusion, to be a monk where life was less stressful. He assumed that monks lived a slow-paced routine in the monastery, doing essentially nothing useful for society and did not contribute positively to the economy of the nation. But Monk Matt definitely did not seem to fit into this perception. Charles thought, *Maybe Matt could work for M-Reality some day.*

What Charles did not know was that Monk Matt had a Master's degree in computer engineering from the University of Michigan. He had worked for ten years after graduation in the aerospace industry, designing aerodynamic simulation software in Detroit. At the age of thirty-two, he returned to Thailand when his mother was very ill. That was when he decided to be ordained as a monk. In Thailand, it is believed that when a son is ordained as a monk, his mother would receive a large merit. Good merits could help a person overcome bad karmic effect. His mother recovered and Matt pledged to be a monk and has been since that time. He dedicated his life to spreading meditation and bring peace to the world. He was currently working on his thesis towards a PhD in World Peace Studies.

Charles jumped in to reply, "That would be a good thing, of course! Who wouldn't want such a cool gadget like AR! It's the latest stuff everyone must have!"

Antonio said, rather sceptically, "Good, I guess, although I don't really update my phone. I am afraid of viruses. So, this AR stuff would not improve my life one bit."

Toby showed a thumbs-up sign. "Yup, agreed, it sounds like a very cool idea. Great! I love my iPhone."

Charles winked at him approvingly.

Theresa shook her head disapprovingly. "It does not do me any good. I love my Samsung and it's not compatible with the Apple iPhone. I am not an iPhone fan and I am not used to it. My Samsung does everything I need for my work. Camera takes great pictures. Also, this new AR stuff could create a terrible situation for me. My nephew would be influenced by this AR stuff, which I don't really know much about. He would pester his father, that is my brother, to buy him the latest phone. Bad idea indeed. Very bad. I might end up buying him the phone instead of his dad because I love my nephew. His dad would never give his son anything. He is a tough cookie and is one of those old-school disciplinarian types."

Monk nodded slowly and said, "So you see, the technology can improve someone's life, or create problems for some parents, or be neutral. When we remove the association of this new technology to anyone, the product stands by itself as just an enhanced product. It's what we call Emptiness. It is neither good nor bad. By itself, it has the potential to be very good for game developers and businesses of online games. Or, potentially, it could be very bad for health and students being distracted from school work.

"We can look at Happiness in the same way. Happiness, by itself, is Empty. But when we associate objects and conditions with Happiness, then it becomes biased. The same actions could make someone very happy and simultaneously cause another someone to be sad. Because everything in our lives is in transition, nothing remains the same. The day we were born, our body started ageing. The concept of Self and impermanence are core foundation principles that affect our state of contentment and happiness."

Antonio wondered how his question about meditation led Monk to talk about self, ego, and happiness. He blurted aloud, "Sorry, Mr. Matt, I am lost. What does self and emptiness have anything to do with meditation?"

Monk explained, "Meditation requires one to let go of one's ego, thoughts, and judgement. The goal of meditation is to achieve Emptiness."

Charles frowned, "So much hard work to get to nothing?"

"Emptiness does not equal Nothingness," said Monk. "Nothingness is devoid of content, whereas Emptiness is devoid of attachment to Self, Identity, and Ego. Let's take the example of a girl being upset with her boyfriend for breaking up with her. She cries, 'Why are you leaving me? What have I done to you?' What do you see in this situation?"

Theresa immediately said, "I see a guy dumping an innocent girl."

Toby countered, "You assume she is the innocent one and he is at fault. I see a girl who feels powerless."

Charles said, "I see a girl in denial by making herself the victim and blaming the boyfriend for her situation".

Antonio turned the situation over in his mind. "I see that the breakup, that is 'leaving me', is an example of an Empty situation. It could be good for both of them to take time off from the relationship. But, because the ego is hurt, and losing something personal is painful, the situation is not Empty anymore. Because they attached 'I', 'me', 'you', and 'why' to the situation, it becomes loaded with emotions and attachment. Hence, it's not empty."

Monk smiled. "You all analysed the situation very well. Antonio is right to identify 'leaving' as a situation of Emptiness. The situation could have a different outcome if the boy considered other factors like the way to let her know, the girl's expectations, how he informed her, and the timing of the announcement. Thus, Nothingness is different from Emptiness. Emptiness refers to the personal and emotional attachments to a situation, an event, or a person, which have the potential to be useful or not useful depending on how we associate our intentions and actions to it. The level of Nothingness, however, refers to how much content is filled into this situation. So, when someone says, "I have no idea this happened, that's why I have no comment about it", he is referring to Nothingness because of the lack of content or awareness of the content. On the other hand, when someone says,

"I know what happened in this situation, but I don't have any opinion about it at this moment", he is referring to a situation which he is currently detached from. This makes the situation Empty, which allows the person to respond to it, perhaps later, with a clearer mindset."

Theresa, still in a reflective mood, reacted, "Being dumped is being dumped. Whichever way you say it, it hurts like hell. But I agree, people need to learn how to break up so that it is less painful. Sigh! I am never going into a relationship again."

Antonio teased, "Don't get attached to that thought. Things are impermanent, so we should allow things to change, and there would be less suffering. Am I right, Mr. Monk?" Antonio was still not comfortable calling Monk Matt in the proper way.

Monk nodded with a non-committal smile. Theresa was not listening as she was deep in the thought about her past failed relationships.

"Okay, I understand that part about Emptiness and attachments. But how do we let go of Ego, Thoughts, and Judgement? It's impossible to stop thinking, even for a second!" exclaimed Charles.

"First, let me talk about Ego," said Monk calmly. "By letting go of 'I' and self-centredness in every thought, every intention, and every action, we will begin the process of disassociation and detachment. Within us, we have an 'Egotistical Mind', or in short the 'Ego-mind', and a 'non-Egotistical Mind', or the 'non-Ego-mind'. When we are faced with a decision, most people respond with self-interest first, before others-interest. Self-interest is caused by the Ego-mind at work. Others-interest is caused by the non-Ego-mind at work. The Ego-mind motivates mankind towards competition, challenges, and expansions. It drives one to climb higher, go further, explore deeper, and achieve more. As humans, we all grew up learning and conditioning ourselves to respond by being protective and defensive. Ironically, the focus of Self-ness makes the mind look outward for answers, whereas the focus of Other-ness makes the mind look inward for meaning to support our actions. Our Ego-mind brings external events into our system and processes these information within us. Our Ego- and non-Ego-minds are constantly engaged in conversations inside our head. They are evaluating, passing judgements, and making decisions. We call this process 'Thinking'. Sometimes the Mind shouts out to us with messages like 'Slow down', 'Be happy', 'I am stressed', 'I cannot take it anymore', 'Go for it!', 'Stop', 'Shoot!', or 'Run!'. We don't know if these messages originate from our Ego- or non-Ego-minds. These messages are what we call 'gut feelings' or 'instincts.'"

Antonio was not convinced. "Ego makes a person strive for excellence and progress, and it create aspirations. It is required for corporate expansion. Without Ego, there would not be ambitions, discoveries, or new inventions."

"Perhaps," said Monk, "the key is to achieve a balance and not let every action to be influenced by our Ego-mind only."

"I understand," said Antonio, feeling a little exasperated. "But how do I get rid of Ego or rather, how do I reduce the influence of Ego? The 'I' is in everything that drives us towards goals and success. Is there a method one can learn to control the Ego?"

Monk sensed the impatience, which was a typical reaction when he interacted with laypeople. They were in a rush and wanted a quick prescription to solving any problem. He answered, "Yes. Ego and self-centredness will go away when we are compassionate and sympathetic of others. The more compassionate and sympathetic we are of others, the more others-ness or selfless-ness we develop and hence, the non-Ego-mind gets awakened, and the Ego-mind goes into 'sleep mode'. We can develop it through meditation as we practise the spirit of sharing loving kindness, which I will show you later. In our normal lives, when we do charity work, give whole-heartedly, without expectation of gratitude, we start practising selflessness. The Ego-mind may try to take credit for every charitable act.

"For example, when we donate something and help others, and we look for acknowledgement or praise, that's Ego at work. When we are charitable but do not seek attention or public visibility for our act of charity, that is non-Ego. In the commercial world, a businessperson would be looking for a return on investments for every dollar invested. This is the natural self-centred response. It is not wrong to expect some return in business because that's what business is about. But, if that behaviour is applied to all activity we do, then self-centredness will eventually lead to excessive desire for material accumulation of wealth and possessions, which is referred more crudely to as Greed, Thirst, or Craving. The opposite of excessive accumulation of things — or taking — is the distribution of things — or giving. By practising more giving away of things — objects, feelings, wealth, friendship, etc — you will reverse the excessive accumulation of things. This will reduce Ego, Self-centredness, and Greed."

Toby mulled on what Monk just said. "So, doing more charitable acts would help to reduce ego and self-centredness. Ok, I understand. How about letting go of thoughts and judgement? That is even more difficult."

"How to let go of thoughts? The technique is to let your mind focus on one simple object so that it does not think other thoughts," said Monk. "The first step is to find a simple mental object that comes to mind easily. An object that it takes little effort for you to visualise."

Antonio started the ball rolling. "This Rolex watch I am wearing. It is my favourite model, the Submariner. I like the logo of a crown on the face of all Rolexes. That's my mental object."

Charles asked, "Could it be my wedding ring? It's been with me for twenty-five years, and it is round with no stones, simple and meaningful."

"My jade pendant from my mum," said Theresa. "I almost lost it once. Now I never let it leave my neck."

"I have nothing." sighed Toby. "Maybe the first trophy from my dance competition when I was seventeen? It's a statue of a dancer with an outstretched hand holding a crystal globe of the world."

Nodding, Monk said, "Now, close your eyes and just imagine this object. Place it in front of your eyes, with your eyes closed. Imagine it floating in front of your face. Breathe slowly and deeply as you allow your mind to focus on this object. You may look at it from the top or from the sides. Think of nothing else except of this object. Let go of any other thought that comes your way. Observe every detail of the object, knowing that later, you are going to draw it from memory. With as little effort as possible, without stress, observe this object. Maintain your breathing, slow and deep. Let the muscles around your eyes relax. Relax the muscles on your face and jaws. Relax your shoulders. Breathe slowly. Continue observing and after three slow, deep breaths, gently open your eyes."

Monk watched the group rub their eyes and stretched their arms. "Did you notice that your mind has fewer thoughts because it is focusing on this object?"

Antonio said, "At first, I was thinking of the time I bought this watch. It was the first $1 million contract that I had won and I bought this watch as a celebration treat for myself. Then my mind was flooded with the happy memories of that moment. When I became aware that I needed to draw it, I began to look carefully into the details of that crown logo only. Soon nothing else mattered as the other thoughts dissipated."

"I had something similar to Antonio's experience," said Charles. "Initially there were good memories of my wedding. I was so young, very happy, but poor. Later, when Monk instructed us to observe it so I could draw it from memory afterwards, my mind switched off every other thought and only focused on the texture and scratches on the gold ring. I even saw it shine brighter and brighter as I focused on it more and more."

Toby shared his expericne. "I just saw the crystal globe. It started to shine bright. I just stared at the light and my mind went blank. Like a bright sun shining at the tip of my hand. I saw the statue as myself, holding that crystal ball."

"That 'blank' experience is close to the Emptiness feeling," said Monk. "When your mind is blank, that's the state we want to get to, where all thoughts stop, and our mind is still. When we see ourselves in a meditative state, it's called awareness. This is a very important step in meditation, to be relaxed as well as aware."

Monk smiled at Toby, thinking that he had the potential to be a good meditator.

Theresa asked, "When we think of memories of our past, how can we stop the mind from doing that? I was flooded by the memories of my mum and some memories were good and some were sad."

Monk replied, "Firstly, when the object reminds us of complex feelings and the past, we should not use that object for meditation, because it adds thoughts to the Mind rather than allowing the Mind to let go. If that's the case, find another simpler object, like a wine glass, the morning sun, a full moon, or just a tennis ball. In my experience, a round sphere like a crystal ball, which is as clear as a polished diamond, is easier for the mind to focus on because it is less complex. With simple shapes and clear objects, the Mind does not have many details to analyse or raise questions. Secondly, our memories are attachment. Attachment to past or future events prevents the Mind from being in the present. Attachments are like heavy anchors that tie the Mind down to a series of thoughts. We need a simple mental object for the Mind to focus on so that it does not get engaged to think of the past or future events."

Charles said, "So, perhaps the wedding ring is not a good idea after all. I am replacing the mental object with a lemon, the kind I use to squeeze for juice every morning. Would that be better?"

"Yes, you may try that," said Monk. "The good thing about meditation is that it's very personal and it takes a little experimentation. Do you remember when you first learnt to ride a bicycle?"

Theresa nodded. "Yes, all I remember was that I fell off the bike a lot, and suffered lots of bruises. But eventually, I was able to balance. I can still remember how I did it. I learnt to ride a bicycle from my father. He held on to the back of my seat while running next to me as I learnt to cycle, balance, and steer. One day, he was running beside me but he never told me that he had let go of the bike, and I thought he was still holding on. So, I just kept riding, thinking that I was safe with Dad holding on to my seat."

Monk smiled, "Yes, meditation is like that. You've got to make some fine adjustments here and there. Use different mental objects. Then you will find that sweet spot where your mind becomes completely still without thought. The moment when you realise that your mind is still, all thoughts will suddenly come rushing back into your mind. But what you had experienced a moment ago before you realised it, is Stillness. That's invaluable! That's success! The key is to maintain it longer each time you meditate."

Toby chuckled and said, "I had something similar to Theresa's cycling experience. It's when I realised that my dad was not holding on to my bike, I wobbled, lost my balance, and fell."

Theresa laughed. "Yes, me too! Mum scolded Dad for letting go. But the truth is I was already able to ride without his help, but needed the confidence that he was holding on."

"Learning to meditate is similar to learning to ride a bicycle," said Monk. "Nobody learns to ride a bicycle by reading a how-to manual. We just watch others do it and instinctively understand a few simple principles of the techniques. No one can explain to you precisely how to maintain balance on a bicycle. You've got to find that sweet spot through experimentation and gaining self-confidence. Your fear will lead you to fall. Your mind is constantly playing tricks on you, talking to you, taking you to places in the past or the future. Your only job is to keep the Mind occupied by focusing on a mental object and nothing else. Eventually, without knowing it, you are free and will start to achieve the perfect balance of Stillness and Awareness."

BELIEF VERSUS TRUTH

By now, Antonio was so engrossed in a mental process to translate meditation into a product which he could introduce to the masses. Charles was imagining himself sitting in a quiet place, atop of a big rock at the apex of a mountain, teaching his team how to meditate, like a Zen master with disciples. Toby's mind drifted into a trance-like daze.

Monk sensed that this was a pivotal moment to push their inquisitive minds further. "Imagine this situation. You encounter someone who claims to have travelled through time from the future. This person shares with you the secret to life that would make you happy forever. However, what he tells you to do is the opposite of what you have been conditioned to do all of your life. Would you believe this person?"

"Yes, why not? He is from the future, right?" said Toby.

Antonio chimed in, "Yes, but only if he can prove that he is real and he can really travel through time. In which case, I really want to patent his time machine!"

Monk went on, "What if this person claims to be the reincarnation of Buddha or Jesus Christ or a Prophet. And this holy man stands in front you now, and he tells you that he has achieved enlightenment and found the truth and the way to achieve happiness. Would people believe him?"

Charles shook his head. "Nope. Never. Without scientific methods, it is not possible for someone like a holy man to discover something that the smartest scientists in the world have not been able to find — the panacea to suffering or the single answer to happiness."

Toby concurred. "That must be a scam and fake. There are lots of fake people around these days."

"Wait, wait..." said Antonio. "If this is a holy man, and he makes sense, I would listen. Hey, it's rare to be able to come close to a Jesus Christ or Buddha. If someone claims to be Christ, and he can perform miracles, I might believe. But only if he shows a few incredible miracles to prove himself."

"What if," said Theresa, "and ignoring proof and other scientific methods... what if he brought information that is really the true answer to life's quest for ultimate happiness? Believing or not does not change the truth. Believing only indicates your own judgement of the truth. If Isaac Newton did not have a way to describe gravity with formulas and measure the gravitational constant as 9.8, does it mean that gravity did not exist before Newton?"

Antonio stared at Theresa with new-found respect at her succinct argument using gravity. Charles squinted his eyes, searching and struggling for a counterargument.

Theresa continued, "Just because we don't see it does not mean it's not there, like air. Yet without air, living things would not survive. Is that invisible thing Air or is it God? Or is it just an oxygen and nitrogen mixture?"

Monk watched with amusement as the four people, who were strangers only 45 minutes ago, engaged each other in philosophical discussions that only best friends would do. He thought that this meeting was not accidental and there was a cosmic reason for this encounter. He believed that the purpose would unveil itself in the future paths ahead.

Monk waited for a lull in the conversation and said, "Now it's time for Monk to ask you a question. Are you content and happy with your lives?"

3

HAPPINESS AND CONTENTMENT

Happiness will never come to those
who fail to appreciate what they already have.
- Buddha -

DRUNK BUT HAPPY

Toby was the first to speak while others struggled to answer Monk's simple question.

"I have always been happy and content with myself when I was very young. But as I grew older, everyone around me never seemed to be satisfied with me. I started to meet everyone's wishes and became increasingly unhappy. My mum expected me to finish college. I was already struggling to complete high school. I wanted to be a dancer just like my dad. I learnt dancing every day at his studio and competed at every local event available. Eventually I became the youth champion of ballroom dancing. Mum wanted me to be a doctor, Dad wanted me to be a dancer. When I completed high school, I started teaching at Dad's studio. I married my dance partner and had three children in succession. Dancing was my passion but managing a dance a studio was not. I did not have time to compete in dance competitions any more because I was constantly conducting dance lessons. My business began to flourish but it made me unhappy. Slowly, drinking became an everyday affair after the studio closed. The business improved, my love for dancing declined, and eventually I started to hate the whole thing."

Theresa nodded her head, looking at Toby with soft compassionate eyes.

Toby glanced at Theresa appreciatively. "My wife ran the business while I focused on teaching. Being the National Champion made my studio a popular choice for dance students. People kept telling me to expand my studio and create a franchise model. They claimed that I could make loads of money. They were right! The more trophies we received, the better the business became. But the more students I trained, the less happy I was. I loved drinking because I didn't have to worry about anything when I was drunk. Eventually, either I was sober and depressed, or I was drunk and happy. My dad sent me to the mental hospital to quit drinking and deal with my depression. One day my wife left me. Most days I slept at the studio drunk and missed my clients' lessons. My wife and father had to cover for me. I didn't have control of my life anymore." Toby looked into the distance and pursed his lips. "So, I decided to pack my bags and travel to Europe for a year. Prague is my first stop and already I have lost my luggage and wallet. Sigh!"

BEING IN CONTROL

Antonio could relate to Toby's story and felt sorry for him. "We only have one life to live. If we don't take control of it, someone else will. My parents did the same thing to me. They wanted me to go to college, to be a lawyer. I attended college but dropped out after the first year to start my first business. When I was in college, I created an online gambling site, which made me a lot of money. But I felt guilty because gambling created a bad habit for people. I then created an online room-matching website for students looking for roommates. I sold it for $10,000 to an employment recruiting agency that modified it into a dating site, which turned out to have three million users within eighteen months. I should have held on to it longer. Next, I created an online stationery website for students to order any type of stationery. I spent $10,000 renting a warehouse to hold the stocks. I hired an administrator to pick stocks and ship them within the same day. It became so successful that we could not keep up with the orders. I sold it to a large traditional stationery retailer for $100,000 and that's where I got my entrepreneur bug. I've never stopped since then. I have two franchise restaurant brands, one business services franchise, and three others which I seeded capital for start-ups focusing on mobile application development."

Theresa interrupted him, "But are you happy? When will you be content?"

Antonio defended himself, "Nobody should be totally contented with himself. Contentment breeds complacency. I feel that I always need to find the next higher mountain to scale. The struggle with the climb may be tough, but reaching the top always made me happy. Sigh! How do you define happiness anyways? It's the journey not the destination. When the going gets tough, the tough get going man!" He was proud of his motivational one liners. Pumping his fist in the air, Antonio continued, "My future is my happiness. When I have a new idea, it sparks a new pursuit of happiness. I guess I am never contented, but I am happy not to be contented. Being discontented spurs me to keep pursuing that unattainable goal of ultimate happiness, that makes me... happy. Does that make sense?"

BEING APPRECIATED

Theresa liked his high energy spirit and chimed in, "I was the same, like you. That's why I became a tour guide. I wanted to see the world and discover corners where history could be retold to enlighten visitors. It's satisfying when the eyes of tourists light up as they learn about history. But… I don't make enough money to travel around the world. I have been in Prague for twelve years and I love the history here. However, the tourists these days are only interested in snapping quick photos with their phones. They are not interested in the history. Am I happy? Hmm… if I have more money I suppose I would get to visit more places and I could be happier. But actually, that would mean being away from home and I will miss Prague. I love living in Prague and I have friends here. I don't know… I am happy sometimes when I get a good tip. I feel valued when a tourist appreciates my services. Other times my life can be quite lonely as a tour guide. But meditation helped me be content with my lifestyle… I guess."

BEING HOME

Charles waited to be last to speak. He wondered if he could trust these people with his private life. But they were just strangers whom he probably would never meet again. So maybe he could reveal a little of his true self. He heaved a deep sigh. "I am not happy at all. I should be happy given my financial position. I live in a large house and own three apartments for rental income. My career is paying for my lifestyle and the cost for my kids to attend international schools. I travel on Business Class, stay in five-star hotels and dine at Michelin-star restaurants. But I feel that I am being pushed along by my own success. I built my career by working harder than my peers. I was always learning and improving myself. I always exceeded my targets and beat my peers in every challenge put forth to me. I don't like to lose. There is no second place. Who remembers the second person who reached Mount Everest?"

Antonio shook his head.

Charles then asked, "Who was the second person who walked on the moon?"

Toby shook his head.

Charles continued, "You see, that's my point! Nobody remembers the person in second place. Some people hated me for my aggressive pursuit of success. But no pain no gain. When I play sports, I play hard. When I work, I work hard. There is no free lunch. People tend to gravitate towards winners and avoid losers, which is aptly described in the Chinese saying 'shengzhe weiwang, baizhe weikou' (胜者为王, 败者为寇). Loosely translated, it means that winners are revered as kings, while losers are despised as lowly paupers. I didn't care if people liked me or not. Eventually, people aligned themselves on my side because of my success. If I failed, even the people who liked me would distance themselves from me. That's the way many people behave in the corporate world. That's reality."

Charles paused, reflecting deeply. "But I cannot get out of my 'wheel of fortune'. The more success I achieved, the more needs I developed and the less time I had left.

I have not spoken to my mum for six months now. I was hardly home for more than two days before I travelled again. The strange thing was, I liked it. Without work I am empty. I am not happy being stuck in this cycle. But retiring is not for me. I cannot do nothing. Believe me, this is the longest time I have ever been by myself without any business associates shuffling papers for my approval and signature. I am sure my mobile phone will be full of messages when I get back since I left it in my hotel room. I aspired to be wealthy so I could retire comfortably. But the more money I earned, the harder it was to retire. My boss wanted me to relocate to Paris to run the EMEA region — that's European, Middle East, and Africa —but that was not where I wanted to be; I wanted to stay in Asia. It is nearer to Japan so I can visit my mother more regularly in Osaka.

I used to think that happiness is achieving an award with a big monetary bonus for an excellent performance. Yes, it was great, but that feeling of euphoria was temporary. Right after that win, the heavy burden followed."

Theresa asked, "And happiness for you is…?"

Charles looked into the distance and thought aloud, "Happiness for me is going home and being able to stay home and relax on the couch with my kids, watching a family movie. That's what makes me happy. However, that never happened. Why? Because I had been travelling so much, the family had gotten into a rhythm of life without me. So, whenever I was home, I felt like a misfit with the family. Of course, they all tried to fit me into their activities, and accommodated me on my choice of movie, but I felt it was not natural. My wife and I hardly have common things to talk about anymore. I guess I am happiest when I am working. At least people need me more. There are targets to achieve and the pressure makes me tick."

Theresa and Toby looked stunned. They were overwhelmed by the misery buried underneath the confidence of this successful corporate executive. All of them just kept very quiet, absorbed in Charles's unhappiness.

Antonio broke the silence. "That's a small price to pay for success. Happiness is creating another venture, and embarking on the journey, then it all leads us back to the same starting block. That's Emptiness right? Err... Monk, what is happiness for you?"

4

HOW TO BE HAPPY

Happiness is not something ready made.
It comes from your own actions.
- Dalai Lama XIV -

LOVE, METTĀ

Monk listened to all their stories sincerely but dispassionately. "In Buddhism, the ultimate state of happiness is Nirvana. It is not easy to use earthly languages to describe Nirvana because it is a celestial experience. Hence, no human language would perfectly do justice to describe it. However, we could describe the stages before we reach Nirvana as the paths that lead us to happiness. The paths consist of prescribed behaviours that we could practise. We need to continue these practices till they become habits. These should not be just one-off exercises but a habitual lifestyle and it will bring perpetual happiness in whatever we do, in this lifetime and beyond other lifetimes through countless rebirths."

They were all listening intently by now. The phrase 'countless rebirths', in particular, captured everyone's interest. Antonio was brought up in the Christian faith. He was taught not believe in reincarnation or rebirth; but being a businessman, he was open to any theories that would help him be a better person. He considered himself a convenient Christian in a business world. What was there to lose by believing?

Charles shifted uncomfortably in his cross-legged position then leaned forward. "Tell us more, please. I think we all need this. How do we practise the path to happiness?" The rest nodded in agreement.

"Firstly, we need to learn to Love," began Monk. "In the Pāli language, Love is called Mettā. Love every living being. Love without desire to possess. No possession and no possessor. Love generously. Love without selection. Love impartially. Love unbiasedly. Even the Bible describes love in a in similar way. Look at 1 Corinthians 13:4–7 where it says, 'Love is patient, love is kind. It does not envy, it does not boast, it is not proud. It does not dishonour others, it is not self-seeking, it is not easily angered, it keeps no record of wrongs. Love does not delight in evil but rejoices with the truth. It always protects, always trusts, always hopes, always perseveres.'

"When you can love people without condition and without expectation of gratitude or reciprocity, that's love in its pure state. When you can do this first step, you will feel a sensation of joy. It is not the same with romantic love. Romantic love is prejudicial and is associated with external physical and experiential attractions."

Turning to all of them, Monk asked, "Can you now think of someone who is close to you and whom you need to give more love to? Someone to love unconditionally, not desiring any gratification, ignoring their past deeds, and just loving them as a good human being? Anyone come to mind?"

Charles blurted, "I love my children. They are everything to me. I love my wife when she is not nagging. But more often these days, we annoy each other a lot. She spends her time gossiping with friends, engaging in things that do not challenge her intellect, like watching Korean TV dramas every day. I think we drifted apart and I don't sense the love I used to have for her."

Monk queried, "The same person we used to love but now, we don't love them in the same way. Why? Did the person change? Did time change? Or did our expectation change?"

Charles reflected on how he used to be attracted to Amy for her chattiness and her ease when mixing with people.

She was smart but not an intellectual, analytical person like him, which is why they were a good match. She laughed easily at his jokes. He appreciated her relaxed style and how she fit into his family so well. She even probably got along with his mum better than Charles did himself.

Toby thought of his dad, who had always been there to support him. When he refused to complete high school, his father hired tuition teachers to help him pull through. He told Toby, "Don't worry about going to university if that's not what you want. Many successful people were college dropouts. But you must complete high school." Why did he hate his father so much recently, even though the old man was the one who pulled him out of alcoholism?

Monk went on, "We tend to associate the object of love with something reciprocal. The object or subject of love must be respectful or meaningful or desirable or worthy. In Mettā, the love is without conditions, without any demand or biases. Look at a cute puppy and we feel love. Look at the eyes of a baby and his tiny face, we feel joy and love. But look at your spouse and you see all the dissatisfaction, events, and behaviours that cloud our minds. Thus, we cannot feel love for them. I know it's not easy. That is why we take small steps on this path."

Theresa reflected aloud, "I am thinking of my mum, whom I loved a lot. But each time I call her, she will nag at me. She will say: 'When are you coming to visit me? Do this, don't do that. Do you have a boyfriend yet? You are not young anymore.' She treats me like a kid. We usually end the phone call angry with each other. How do I love her if she keeps pressing all my buttons?"

Toby agreed, "Yeah, that pretty much describes my parents, times ten! I don't like going home. When I do, I just stay in my room."

Antonio said, "I love my customers. They are the reason my businesses are successful. It's in my corporate mission: 'The Customer is King'. Is that love?" He smirked, looking for approval from the Monk.

"If we have difficulty loving the people closest to us," said Monk, "perhaps it might be easier to love ourselves first, then spread that loving kindness to those we love, and then spread to include others. Love all living beings that we don't know at all, like everyone in this park. Our hearts need to be softened to begin to love again, like an innocent child who trusted and loved anyone who cared for him. The children we were then grew up to be sceptical and careful of whom we love because adults have programmed us with advice like 'Don't trust strangers'; 'Don't believe the stories from Uncle Bob. He's a loser'; 'Nothing is free. You've got to pay for it, one way or another'. Over time, these advice had hardened our hearts and we lost our innocence and became judgemental. We trusted ourselves more than others. That's why the world is facing so many problems today.

"Some people look at churches or temples as profit-generating institutions and lose faith. When people lose faith in religion, they only trust themselves. Believing in ourselves creates an egocentric society. What we believe may not be the truth. Yet perception is reality. Our reality is influenced by our past experiences, our philosophies and values. **When we trust only our own reality, we stop seeking the truth.** We become tunnel-visioned to find evidence to support our beliefs. Psychologists call this belief-biases. We live in our own perceptions of truth. We need to open our hearts to see and accept the truth. We are losing the act of loving kindness in this world. It is not just love between two persons in a relationship. It's Mettā. It's love without possessor, without possession. Its loving kindness."

Charles jumped in, "Okay, okay. This is good stuff. I like it. Assume I am willing to withhold my judgement for now and I am open to embracing Mettā. Can you teach us how to do it? I mean how to love unconditionally?" Theresa, Toby, and Antonio nodded in agreement. They all leaned forward, waiting for more from the Monk.

Monk looked around the park, noticing people enjoying themselves. Dogs were walking beside their owners. Some kids were throwing a frisbee. What a nice place to spend the day! Everyone followed Monk's eyes as if directed by an invisible instruction to mirror his actions. Toby soon noticed that Charles's face brightened, and Antonio's breathing slowed and the frown on his face dissolved into a smile. He watched as Theresa smiled and stretched her neck as she released her hair, letting it hang loose on her shoulders. Everyone looked more relaxed. Toby felt a peaceful feeling engulf his entire body.

Monk instructed, "Look in front of you. With your eyes open, breathe in deeply and slowly. Breathe in... Breathe out... Breathe in... Breathe out... Continue to breathe slowly, without force, just naturally."

Monk watched as the group followed his directions. "With each breath, feel the muscles of your body relaxing."

Monk's voice was calm and low. "Be aware of the muscles on your forehead. Relax them. The muscles at the corners of your eyes — relax them. Relax your facial muscles and allow your jaws to relax. You may maintain a slight smile on your lips, as smiling relaxes the muscles on your face."

Monk paused to allow the group to relax and be aware of their bodies.

"Relax the neck and shoulders... your arms, your chest, torso, and hip. Be aware of your leg muscles, feel it touching the ground you are resting on. Relax."

Monk paused again, allowing the group to follow him. He did not want to rush them.

"Slowly allow your eyelids to close ever so gently. Do not squeeze your eyes shut. Just gently allow the lids to touch and if you see some light coming through the gap, it's alright. If you see darkness, it's alright. Just be comfortable and relax."

The sound of birds chirping in the distance could be heard. Also the sounds of happy laughter coming from the kids playing, and pebbles crunching as the rubber wheels of bicycles rolled along the paths. The distant sounds of bells echoed through the air as watergates opened and closed along the river.

"You may notice the rhythm of your breathing getting shallower and slower. Slowly bring your awareness inside your body and allow each breath to bring in cool and fresh air into the body. Imagine every cell in your body smiling happily and enjoying the fresh air inside the body. Relax. You may be aware of some sounds around you. These sounds will get softer and softer as you focus inner and inner into your body. With no effort at all, bring your focus inside your body. Relax the muscles at the corners of your eyes. Continue to breathe slowly, in and out in a slow rhythm. Your mind may wander around, with thoughts bringing you away from the present. This is normal. Don't fight it. When you are relaxed, the mind will come back because it's comfortable here. Just focus on the gentle breathing rhythm. Relax while maintaining the gentle smile on your face."

Monk allowed the group to meditate for about a minute in silence before easing in softly with more instructions.

"Relaaaaxxx... Relaaax... Relaaaax... You may begin to feel the lightness of your body. Some of you may feel warmer because of the sensation of your body heat. Slowly spread your feeling of loving kindness to people around you. From the centre of your stomach, imagine a glowing ball expanding its light outwards from your body.

Your loving kindness is like the light spreading away from the centre of your body. Just like an ice cube, spreading its coolness into the environment around it. Spread your good feelings, relaxing feelings, and feelings of lightness to people around you. Spread it wider and wider, around this tree, and spreading wider to the park. Spread it as far as you can reach. Feel positive, calm, light, and relaxed. Continue doing this with no effort or force. Relax. If the image of any persons or characters comes into your mind's eye, spread this loving and kind feeling to them, generously and unconditionally. Relaaaax..."

The group sat in silence for a few more minutes. The cool breeze continued to waft in their direction. Horns from distant boats could be heard from the river.

"Breathe in... and out... Slowly increase the breathing deeper and deeper into your abdomen and chest. Breathe in... Breathe out... Take three more breaths and when you are ready, slowly allow your eyes to open."

Monk waited for each of them to open their eyes. All of them had a serene look. Monk smiled and look at them. "Congratulations! You have just completed your first meditation class and the sensation of loving kindness."

Antonio was still in half a daze. He shook his head and brightened up. "Wow! That. Was. So. Cool. I mean it was so relaxing. I felt my body floating and didn't want to get out of it when you said to open our eyes."

Toby looked at his watch. "Whoa!, Did we just spend 15 minutes in meditation?"

Charles was surprised. "Really? That could not be. I felt it was just a few minutes. But I felt so... so... relaxed."

Theresa was smiling and kept quiet. She was a regular meditator so she understood the feeling. She was surprised how the Monk just led the group into meditation without informing them that he was going to do it. Yet everyone just followed his instructions. At that moment, she knew that the Abbot had sent the right monk to Prague. He would do a great job with the ten-day workshop for the Prague Peace Revolution group.

Monk said, in a serene, low and calm voice, "What you felt was what some people call happiness. Others call it relaxing. Some even call it the sense of lightness. It could also be called the sensation of Loving Kindness. Whatever language you use to describe it, did it feel good?"

Everyone nodded.

Charles said, "When you asked us to spread loving kindness, I saw my wife's image, and I looked at her with neutral emotions. She was just a person and because I did not see her with all the burdens of being my wife, I was able to spread my happiness to her. I even wished her happiness as well... from my mind, of course. Is that Mettā... Love?"

Monk maintained a calm voice, but inside him, he was excited that Charles made a connection to Mettā. "People experience meditation differently. Some feel physical relaxation, some get deeper insights into things they could not see before, others take a longer time to get inner experiences. It all depends on their state of mind. How did it feel to have that experience?"

Charles's eyes looked up, scanned left and right, then he looked down towards his right foot, breathing in and out, as if reflecting on his experience. "Good. I felt very peaceful and neutral. The strange thing is, I did not pass any judgement on my wife. I saw her with a radiant glow as if there was an bluish white aura around her."

Toby and Antonio were amazed by Charles's experience. They looked at him and then looked back at Monk, wanting to see his reaction. Monk smiled gently, without expressing any excitement or emotion. "That's good. Keep doing that. We call that Loving Kindness. When you were able to feel that and share that with others, you nurture a purer mind. With a purer mind, you will be more willing to see the purity in others. Hence it will get easier and easier to love. When our minds are clouded or defiled with judgements, opinions, and emotions, we can only see the dark side of others. Charles, you are able to have this experience because you have meditated before in your past lifetimes. This is not your first meditation experience."

Charles had never meditated before, but he smiled, feeling proud of his achievement. He felt special. And Monk's comment of his past life intrigued him. He wanted to explore that topic deeper, later when he had time with Monk. He thought: *I need to engage this monk to conduct a workshop for my team.*

Monk turned to look Toby and Antonio, and saw their jaws slightly opened in amazement at Charles's experience. Monk's eyes stopped at Antonio "How did you feel with this meditation?"

Antonio eyes looked down at his toes as he searched for a way to describe his experience. "I cannot describe it. It was a strange feeling… of nothingness. At first I felt the cold air, then the noise of dogs barking and sounds of birds became louder than before. Then when I focused on my breathing, these noises started to become distant and eventually, they did not even disturb me at all. All I felt was alone and calm. But my thoughts were wild. I came up with so many ideas for my business. I realised that I was probably starting too many businesses and not spending enough time to develop each one properly. I wanted to write down all these ideas, but I didn't want to stop the flow of thoughts. Even though there were lots of thoughts, my mind also felt clearer and better able to discern what was useful and what was rubbish. Why is that, Monk?"

Monk asked, "How did you feel about that experience?"

Antonio grinned, "Actually, I've never been more relaxed than this before. I did not feel overwhelmed. I felt calm and serene. Good feeling!"

Monk smiled in return. "That's good. During meditation, when the body is relaxed, the mind starts to settle down. Initially, the mind will wander all over. As you begin to be more and more relaxed, the mind will start to filter the information, some to focus on and others to ignore. At some stage — and it's different for different people — some thoughts may appear clearer. Some people have found answers in the clutter of random thoughts because a mind that is at a standstill can pick up valuable gems from the cloudiness. It's called clarity. The answer had probably been there all the time, but the mind was so busy that it did not see it before. Breathing helps to settle the mind. Thoughts start to dissolve and the mind begins to be stiller and stiller. A mind that is at a complete standstill will develop a power and wisdom. Through practice, you can maintain the same state of stillness of the mind while engaging in daily activities. You will make better decisions in normal daily work. That's why we keep meditating, and keep practising daily to nurture the mind, and not to be like a monkey jumping from tree to tree. A monkey mind is a wandering mind. A mind that is at a standstill is where inner wisdom and power can be attained."

Toby laughed loudly, "Ha! Ha! Ha! Monkey mind... I like that description. It is so true. My mind was all over the place. I had so many thoughts of my past. My mind was reflecting past events that reminded me of guilt, regrets, and joy — all playing in front of my eyes like a movie. At first, I was very disturbed by it, so I repeatedly breathed in and out, telling myself to relax my facial muscles and the areas around my eyes. After a while, the movie started to slow down and went into a blurry image. Then suddenly, I saw a bright white light. It was very bright like the midday sun. I kept looking at it and started to feel it pulsating, and it kept to the rhythm of my heartbeat. Then I felt warm all over my body. And it stayed that way till I opened my eyes."

Monk smiled and nodded, "The warmth comes from inside your body. You felt warm because your mind is inside your body. The sphere of bright light is a good progress. Besides the warmth, how did you feel overall?"

Toby wriggled his body and stretched his neck left and right. "I felt very relaxed. And I felt good — like a floating feeling. I felt like I was dancing… ballroom dancing all alone. So free and so not limited by boundaries. But how do I stop my mind from wandering all over?"

Monk held up a glass of water to his eye level. "Imagine this glass is your mind. The content is crystal clear spring water. Thoughts of the past are like suspended powder that has settled at the bottom of the glass. When we stir the glass, these suspended particles start to cloud the clear water. A wandering mind is one that is being stirred. When we are worried, angry, busy, rushing to meet deadlines, we are stirring the water. A busy person will take a longer time to settle his mind, just like a glass of stirred water needs to sit still longer on the table before the suspended particles settle to the bottom. Meditation gives your mind a chance to sit still, to allow these particles to settle to the bottom. So, in order to stop the mind from wandering, we should give it time to settle down. We can also do some stretching exercises so the mind is not thinking about the leg muscles or tight clothing. A nice and cool environment also removes any distraction that could stir the mind. Telling yourself to ignore the outside world and focus on the inside world of your body may help. Another technique to stop the mind wandering is to let the mind think of one object, like a crystal ball or a diamond ball, so it focuses on only one thing and not many things."

Theresa looked calm and collected. But the three guys looked at her expecting her to say something. She looked back and shrugged her shoulders, "Cool stuff guys. It took me months of meditating to experience what you all got today. You should all keep doing it. Don't waste that ability."

The three men just looked back at her feeling good.

COMPASSION, KARUNĀ

Monk continued, "There are four paths you should know on your journey to Happiness. You have experienced Loving Kindness during meditation, that's the first path. The second path is Compassion, or Karunā in Pāli. Compassion is made up of two words: 'com' meaning together and 'passion' meaning a strong feeling. When we see someone in distress and we feel his pain as if it were our own, then strive to eliminate or lessen that pain, that is Compassion. So, all the best in human beings, all the qualities like sharing, readiness to give comfort, sympathy, concern, and caring — all these are manifestations of compassion. You will notice also that in the compassionate person, care and love towards others have its origins in care and love for oneself. We can really understand others when we really understand ourselves. We will know what's best for others when we know what's best for ourselves. We can feel for others when we feel for ourselves. So regardless of which religion one follows, one's own spiritual development blossoms quite naturally into concern for the welfare of others."

SYMPATHETIC JOY, MUDITĀ

"The third path is Sympathetic Joy or Muditā, in Pāli language," said Monk. "When we rejoice at the good fortune of others, it leads to Joy. The opposite experiences of Joy are Jealousy and Envy. When someone, particularly your competitor, wins a deal or receives an award which you think should be yours, how would you react?"

Antonio admitted, "I usually become very disappointed with myself. And sometimes upset that they won, and occasionally suspect that they bribed the judges or cheated. I may not express these feelings outwardly, but I cannot control myself from entertaining these thoughts of envy and jealousy, like a sore-loser mindset. I won't show displeasure openly, of course, but inside my quiet self, I would be pissed like hell. Oops, sorry, I mean upset."

Monk said, "You are right. Sympathetic Joy is the experience of being happy for the success of others instead of being jealous or envious of others. To practise inner joy, we need to have thoughts and acts of rejoicing in the success and happiness of others and congratulating them sincerely. By just thinking of rejoicing or of being envious already creates an intention, which could lead us to committing a karmic action. The ill-willed intention does not generate karma effect yet. However, thinking creates an intention, and usually leads to an action, which has either a good karma or bad karma consequence."

Charles was not convinced. "In the corporate world, if a co-worker got the promotion that we were both competing for, how could I rejoice in their success? That's so... so... unnatural. Externally, I can congratulate him in front of the company. But inside my heart, how can I not be disappointed, angry, or jealous? And for other teams who win the best team award, how can I stop my mind from being envious? Usually, as a response, I will challenge my team to beat them the next year. Using envy as a motivator to drive positive improvement, that should be good right?"

Toby chimed in, "I can see how losing to the competition can spur the team to work harder. We can build on the emotions of Jealousy and Envy to motivate ourselves to do better next time. I used that kind of motivation a lot when training dancers for competition. It works for some people, but not for everyone. But, isn't that good?"

Antonio agreed, "Yeah, I use another's failure as a lesson for us to learn what to avoid, and their success as our inspiration and role model."

"To want to improve is a good attitude," said Monk. "However, within our minds and hearts, there is a long-term negative effect when we use negative energy to create unwholesome thoughts to motivate ourselves to strive for improvement. Unwholesome thoughts include envy, jealousy, anger, revenge, spite, sarcasm, hatred."

Toby thought about his own dance competitions. It was competitive pressure that drove him to win. Losing was not an option for him, so he struggled to agree with this Sympathetic Joy concept. "But Matt... er.. Monk... er... Monk Matt, competition is good. It pushes one to stretch to one's potential. Innovation is also created out of the pressure of necessity. So why is it not good?"

Monk explained, "When we avoid jealousy and envy and eliminate the sour-loser mindset, we look for other areas of motivation. When we meditate, the practice of sharing Loving Kindness will soften our inner mind. Softening of the mind does not weaken the mind. It actually strengthens the mind with an inner power that negates the dark energy of anger, jealousy, or envy. Through loving kindness, we will eventually learn to replace these sore-loser feelings with feelings of joy for our competitors and rejoicing in their success through congratulations and genuine wishes. When our joyful mind makes wishes for ourselves, the karmic effect will work in our favour. A good karma starts with a good intention, which could be as simple as a thought. If we think well of ourselves and of others, our hearts and minds will be more generous and compassionate. This will bring more Joy, and the result of these karma will be more success for ourselves in the future."

"Wow! That's a lot of deep stuff to digest," said Toby. "Let me see if I remember them. The paths to happiness are firstly, Loving Kindness. It's non-biased, unconditional, impartial, not selective, and to be felt towards all living beings. And the more we share this Loving Kindness, the softer the minds and hearts get. And the softer mind is a more powerful mind; it is not weaker. The second path is.. umm… the second is…"

Antonio jumped in, "…is Compassion. Being compassionate is to feel for the suffering of others' pain. Feeling another's pain will bring out the best human qualities of sympathy, concern, caring, and sharing. When one loves oneself, one will love others, and extend one's compassion towards them. I think it also works the other way as well. That is, when one loves others, one will begin to love oneself as well. Compassion brings more love and hence, more joy and happiness."

Charles did not want to lose out as a star student, so he added, "The third path is Joy, Sympathetic Joy. That's the act and thought of rejoicing in others' success. It's the feeling of happiness for others when they win or achieve something. The opposite of Joy are the negative emotions of jealousy and being envious of others' success. Some other negative emotions that are the opposite of joy are vengeance, cruelty, hatred, and sarcasm. When we practise this path of Joy, our Mind gets more generous and kind."

Cheekily, Antonio said, "I think Compassion is the most powerful of these three paths."

Theresa frowned and quipped, "Hey Antonio, it is not a competition. All three paths are equally needed toward the attainment of happiness."

Antonio smiled, "It's a joke, Theresa!"

Toby and Charles laughed, then Toby asked, "What is the fourth path?"

EQUANIMITY, UPEKKHĀ

Monk said, "The fourth path is Equanimity, which has been translated into two Pāli words: Upekkhā which means 'to look over' and Tatramajjhattata which means 'there'. It is the ability to be **Involved with indifference** at the same time. And to be **Interested with dispassion** concurrently. For example, at the passing of a loved one, an equanimous attitude would be to feel the loss and have the awareness of the person's transcendence to a better place. The sense of sorrow arising could be loss, guilt, anger, or sadness. At the same time, the sense of relief arising could be to rejoice for the end of the suffering. To be equanimous in such situations is to remain mindful of the feelings from the past, mixed emotions of the present, the uncertainty of the future, and yet not be affected by any one state."

Monk concluded, "When you practise the four paths of Love, Compassion, Joy, and Equanimity, you are heading in the right direction towards Happiness. Any other questions?"

Charles, Antonio, and Toby all raised their hands together. Theresa looked nervously at her watch. Monk looked at them patiently, encouraging them to ask.

SINS, KARMA, AND HEAVEN

Charles started the ball rolling. "This is good. Now, I have a methodology to be happy. Meditation clears the mind. Sympathy and Compassion condition the Mind to be softer and kinder. But, how do I balance the demands of the real world where we are faced with distractions and temptations with the practices required by these four paths? I mean, can a person be successful, as defined by wealth and materialism, and still achieve happiness? We don't have to give up our lifestyle to be a monk in order to achieve happiness, right?"

"Great question!" said Monk, then turned to Antonio, "And your question?"

Antonio replied, "I am a Christian and we believe that everyone is born a sinner. Christ's death cleansed all our sins which gave us a chance to go to heaven and have eternal life, at least that's what Sunday school taught me. But I've also heard about karma. Is that similar to sins? Can good karma negate bad karma? Karma logic is based on the belief of reincarnation. As Christians, we are told that there is no such thing as reincarnation. So now, I don't know what to believe."

As Monk nodded, Toby said, "My question is simple… If I die, how do I know I will go to heaven?"

Theresa thought these were great questions and used it as a segway to interject, "Excuse me, Monk Matt, you have to be at the next meeting by 3 p.m. We need to leave soon."

Monk acknowledged with a nod, then turned to the three men. "These are all great questions. In fact, tonight, I am giving a talk about these topics, 'Karma and the Effect on Our Lives Here and After' and 'The Three Poisons: Greed, Anger, and Delusion'. Greed represents attachment to material gains like money, houses, big cars, mobile phones, toys, etc. These are all associated with the accumulation of worldly wealth or material things. Anger represents the physical senses that lead to desires. Desires are feelings of pleasure, enjoyment, sensual pleasure, guilt, sadness, anger, vengeance, and other emotions. When we are detached from the six senses of sight, smell, hearing, taste, touch, and thought, we begin to take control of our Mind, instead of letting the Mind control us. Delusion refers to the states of ignorance, knowledge, wisdom, and awareness. Not knowing is not an excuse for committing an offence. Knowing is knowledge, and acting on the knowledge is Wisdom. What you believe and what you want to believe is entirely up to you. But Believing does not mean it is real or it is true. Believing is your perception of reality. And that perception may not be the truth. You've got to discover for yourself whether karma is real, or rebirth is real. Did Buddha exist? Did Jesus resurrect from death? How do you know? Ehipassiko! That is a Pāli word for 'come, see or find out for yourself.'"

Theresa said, "If you could join us, you will find out more about these topics. Monk Matt will teach meditation as well. So, you will get 2-in-1 package by attending the talk tonight. I will reserve front row seats for you."

Monk thanked the group as they dispersed. "I wish to see you at the workshop tonight. May you find your inner peace. May you continue to meditate and achieve your one-ness of mind, body, and soul."

The group dispersed except for Charles. He wanted to know if Monk could spare 30 minutes to address his team tomorrow morning, at the closing of his sales meeting. Monk said, "Sure, come to the session tonight. Let's see how Theresa can rearrange my schedule to fit that in."

5

ANGER AND HATRED

When all else fails, there's always delusion.
- Conan O'Brien -

THE CEO

The meeting with the Monk at the park made Charles think about how he had led his life. He had a natural introspective nature and he often challenged himself to find a balance between work and family. To him, family was the most important priority in his life; yet, his career had taken him further away from his mum, his siblings, and his time with his two growing children of ten and fourteen years of age. While walking back to the hotel, his mind was bombarded by these questions: *Am I truly happy? What can I do to be truly happy and still build a successful career? Do I have to give up my career, or slow down, in order to achieve true happiness? I love Amy, but why don't I feel the love the same way as before? How much money is enough for me to retire? What happens if I only have thirty days to live? What would I do? How would I want to be remembered? Monk said there are 'countless lifetimes'. Does that mean I will go to another life after I die? What's that? And how do I prepare for the next life?*

Charles Takashi Watanabe was a senior executive responsible for M-Reality's regional business in Asia Pacific and Japan. He was a self-proclaimed workaholic. He graduated with a first-class honours degree in computer science, worked from the position of programmer to Regional Area Vice President of Asia. That was a steep ladder to success. Essentially, he was the CEO of this business division, or the head honcho in this region. Charles's family was everything he worked for. He tried to maintain a good balance between family and career; but he had to grade himself a C-minus. His wife, Amy, gave up her career at Anders Consulting to join Charles when he was relocated to Singapore. It was a good decision as she could focus on nurturing their two children as they continued their education at an international school in Singapore.

His relationship with his wife lacked the spark it used to have. They still loved each other but these days, when they were together, their relationship was mostly perfunctory. This could have been caused by Charles's fast-tracked career since moving to Singapore. Charles had accumulated a personal wealth and asset of almost $20 million in net worth. He was working on creating a trust to ring-fence his asset in stocks, properties, and cash so that the family would get a fair distribution with minimal tax burden. He was willing to give everything to Amy and his two children when he left this world.

Charles's relationship with his two kids was great. He had always tried his best to play the role of a good father to compensate for his personal lack of a father due to his parents' separation at the age of five. He and Amy kept their disagreements under wraps and nobody except their closest friends knew about their challenges. The undercurrents of their relationship were stirring beneath while calmness showed on the surface.

Charles went back to his meeting after the brief encounter with the Monk at the park. He was more relaxed after meditating and he seemed clearer about the need to prioritise his life. He did not pay attention during the product presentations and demonstrations on stage. Usually this was the part of the afternoon where the Product Managers would excite the audience with upcoming products and their cool features. Today, Charles had a different plan. He wrote on his note pad:

✓ Happiness is a journey not a destination.
✓ Share Love. Unconditional. Impartial. No possession no possessor. Non-selective.
✓ Sympathetic Joy. Be happy with success of others. Rejoice in their merits.
✓ Compassion. Feel the misfortune of others. Help them.
✓ Keep things simple. Simplify life. Fewer possessions. Minimal living.
✓ Mindfulness. Meditate more. Be present.

Charles loved projects, so he listed each of his actions as a 'project' and even committed dates to these.

Today is the first day of a new life:
To be Successful and Happy

Actions:
1. Project Mettā   Call Mum. Tell her I love her.
                         Date: Next week
2. Project Mettā   Call Amy. Tell her the things I
                         appreciate about her.
                         Date: Next week
3. Project Compassion   Check on Toby. He is in a difficult
                         situation. Maybe I can help.
                         Date: Tomorrow
4. Project Meditate   Check for classes in Singapore.
                         Date: Start soon

5. Project Simplify   To reduce old stuff I don't need.
                         Give away or have a garage sale till
                         I get rid of all extras.
                         Date: Start next month
6.

He paused and thought hard before writing point 6. Charles closed his eyes, breathed slowly, and visualised. He frowned and his face contorted into a grimace. As his breathing slowed down, his face relaxed, and a slight smile appeared. Then the smile broadened into a wider grin. He opened his eyes and beamed, then shook his head, saying to himself, *I can't believe I am doing this. I am going to do it.* He wrote:

6. To quit my corporate job. Retire from M-Reality by 31 Dec, three years from today

Charles felt good after writing his commitments down. The product demo had just finished and everyone was cheering and clapping. People loved the product demonstrations. Charles looked at the last part of the latest software demo and thought that it was pretty cool and had potential. The announcer then invited everyone for evening cocktails at 6 p.m. at the lobby bar, before the bus that would take everyone to the Palace for dinner would leave at 7 p.m. Just then, Charles received a text from an unknown number: 'Charles, the talk by Monk Matt starts at 8 p.m.

Have reserved a good seat for you. Meet 7.30 p.m. at Mala Strana Square. Walk there together. Toby and Antonio are coming too. Please confirm ASAP. Theresa'.

Charles was wondering how he could escape the group dinner. He really wanted to attend the Monk's talk, but he was expected to give a speech and hand out some Sales Excellence awards. He felt a tap on his shoulders. Turning around instinctively, he saw Ted who is the Vice President of International Sales and his boss, looking at him with a wide grin. "Hey Charles, didn't see you at lunch. Where did you sneak off to? Went shopping?"

Charles gave a frown in reply. "Nah, I went for a walk at the nearby park. Talking about shopping, I don't know about women these days and crystals. I already have Bohemian crystals flowing out of my ears at home, yet Amy wants me to buy another vase for the living room. Sigh!"

Ted laughed, "At least she didn't ask you for a diamond! The secret to a happy relationship is to keep the wife and her mother happy. As long as she is happy, give her two vases! One for her mother too. Your region will receive a few awards at dinner tonight. You should be happy. Great year!"

Charles recalled the Monk's question, "Are you happy with your life?" He punched Ted lightly on the arm and with an assuring smile said, "Sure, Ted. Of course! We worked hard for the year!"

Then he went over to Shirley, the events programme coordinator. She used to work for him before he promoted and moved her to the marketing team. He knew he could influence her to adjust tonight's programme schedule to put his awards ceremony upfront. He lied that he needed to have a conference call with the US at 8 p.m. "I must leave by 7.55 p.m. at the latest, okay?" Charles pleaded. Shirley winked and replied, "Sure, boss. Anything for you, boss!"

Charles texted Theresa: 'Hi Theresa. Thanks for the invite. I can only be there at 8.30 p.m. Have a group dinner that I need to attend. I can only leave by 8 p.m. Please give location address — I will make my way there myself. Keep a seat for me, please. Thanks!'

Subsequently, Theresa texted him the address of the meeting. Coincidentally, it was at the old monastery which was just a 5-minute walk up the hill from the restaurant he would be at. Charles was happy with the arrangement. He would do the award presentation upfront, then have some team photos taken. After that he would disappear to attend the Monk's talk. By 9 p.m., the talk should be done. He would sneak back to the dinner and people would still be networking till 10 p.m. *They won't miss me*, he thought optimistically.

THE ENTREPRENEUR

When Antonio left the meeting with Monk at Kampa Park, he knew immediately that his life needed to change. *But, how to?* he thought. That evening, he attended the talk by

Monk Matt and that session provided him with the 'how to' to make those changes. He recalled a few key messages from Monk's talk on Anger, Greed, and Delusion. The part that woke him up was about his anger and emotions. He realised that he did not have many real friends; yet, many people admired and respected his work. He was very good at building businesses, by taking ideas from conceptualisation to execution. Most of the time he made them work when others failed. His attitude of 'Failure is not an option' drove his team nuts; yet, at the end of the day, it worked. 'Take no prisoners' was another of his well-known mantras. Antonio was very goal-oriented and he showed little sympathy for inefficiency and incompetency. He often told project teams, "I hate stupidity and people who don't think. People who don't use their brains should not exist at all!" Many of his followers were action-oriented, self-critical, competitive, and aimed for perfection. They fired people who didn't perform. Their teams had been indoctrinated by his work culture of: 'Got to get it right the first time. People only remember the winners not the losers. We don't always get a second chance.'

Antonio realised that his success formula made him impatient, angry, and discontent with anything and anyone, anywhere. In his personal life, he never stayed in any relationship long enough to call it a relationship. Some were as brief as just a conversation. No one was good enough in his eyes. He remembered Monk asking. "At the finish line, who will be there to meet you? When your career is over, when you retire from your company, and all the parties are over, who will be out there to meet you and who will go home with you?" Antonio could not come up with an answer.

Antonio felt a wave of sadness when he reflected on his life and all he saw was emptiness. He was always driving people hard and people were just numbers and components in his grand plans. If he died in a plane crash, many people would be affected by the loss of the businesses that he had built, but very few would be affected by the loss of his friendship, personal or business. Antonio suddenly felt a sense of lonely emptiness inside his heart. He reflected on the section of Monk's talk when he spoke about Anger.

THE MONK'S TALK

Monk Matt asked the audience, "What's the opposite of Anger?"

Many members of the audience raised their hands to offer their answers to Monk's question. One said, "Happiness."

"No," said another, "Happiness is the opposite of Sadness. The opposite of Anger is Peace."

Yet another person interjected, "No. Peace is the opposite of War. The opposite of Anger is Love."

"That's not right," said a fourth person. "The opposite of Love is Hate. The opposite of Anger has to be Contentment."

"But the opposite of Contentment is Craving and Desires," a young man called out. "The opposite of Anger should be Equanimity."

Monk gestured for the audience to calm down. "There are so many different answers depending on who you ask and the context. There is no simple opposite to Anger. Anger is one emotion that is represented by feelings of hatred, dissatisfaction, discontent, rage, vengeance, aversion, and many more. Anger does not contribute positive value to the person expressing it nor the person receiving it. Anger emits a high level of negative feelings and dark consciousness. This level of consciousness can be destructive. Sometimes, it can be the motivator for a person to overcome major hurdles in his life. But using Anger as a motivator to change will perpetuate the outcome with more anger.

"For example, soldiers who were filled with hatred for the opposing forces used this energy to destroy their enemies just to win the battle. At the end of the battle, the soldiers would still be filled with hatred and anger. Some of this anger could turn into remorse, guilt, shame, or fear. The victory was not sweet."

Monk continued, "Anger is associated with the emotions of hatred. And these revolve around the feelings of guilt, shame, and desires. Desires are caused by our senses of touch, thought, sight, hearing, smell, and taste. The pleasures associated with these senses create desires, which cause us to want more. These sensations can be pleasurable or non-pleasurable. It can also show up as anger, hostility, dislike, aversion, or ill-will resulting in one person wishing harm or suffering upon another person.

"With aversion, we habitually resist, deny, and avoid people we dislike, or avoid unpleasant feelings and circumstances. We want everything to be pleasant, comfortable, and satisfying all the time. Because everything changes and nothing is permanent, these desires for pleasurable senses will stop and eventually lead to negative emotions.

"These behaviours simply reinforce our perception of duality, like right or wrong, black or white, good or evil. Hatred and anger thrust us into a vicious cycle where the mind looks for conflicts and enemies everywhere and all around us. When there are conflicts or perceived enemies around us, the mind becomes neurotic and never stays calm. We become obsessed with strategies of self-protection or revenge.

"The mind can also find conflicts within ourselves. This happens when we have an aversion to our own uncomfortable feelings. With hatred and aversion, we deny, resist, and push away our own inner feelings of fear, hurt, or loneliness. We treat these feelings like an internal enemy. Hatred causes the mind to create conflicts and enemies not only in the world around us but also within our own being."

Monk went on to tell the story of a boy who was always angry. "Once upon a time, there was a little boy with a bad temper. His father gave him a bag of nails and told him that every time he lost his temper, he should hammer a nail in the fence. By the end of the first week, the boy had driven thirty-seven nails into the fence. But gradually, the number of daily nails dwindled down. He discovered it was easier to hold his temper than to drive those nails into the fence.

Finally, the day came when the boy didn't lose his temper at all. He proudly told his father about it. The father then suggested that the boy now pull out one nail for each day that he was able to hold his temper. The days passed and the young boy was finally able to tell his father that all the nails were gone. The father then took his son by the hand and led him to the fence and said, "You have done well, my son, but look at the holes in the fence. The fence will never be the same. When you say things in anger, they leave scars just like the holes in this fence. You can hurt someone with angry words and apologise afterwards. However, it won't matter how many times you say you're sorry, the wound is still there."

Monk ended this section with a quote from Lord Buddha: 'Holding on to anger is like grasping a hot coal with the intent of throwing it at someone else; you are the one who gets burned.'

At the end of the talk, Antonio knew what he had to do. He scribbled in his notebook:

1. Start living in the Present. Do not live in the future all the time. Focus on making the existing businesses great instead of adding new ventures.
2. Escape from this 'sense-pleasure' cycle. Find the power within myself. Do not rely only on the force of financial success to get results. Maybe, learn meditation? Or yoga? Or other means to seek inner peace and happiness?
3. Do not be angry all the time. How? To ask Monk for advice after the workshop.

Antonio had stayed till the end of the session to ask Monk some questions. There were many people waiting to speak with him, so Antonio asked Theresa if he could have a one-on-one session with Monk. With a twinkle in her eye, Theresa asked, "How early can you wake up?"

Antonio frowned and grimaced. "Oh… I am not a morning person." Then he said, "But I really want to meet Mr. Monk. I have a few tough questions I need answers for. Tell me how early, and I will make it."

Theresa gave Antonio a wicked look. "Okay, how about 6.15 a.m.? Monk finishes his morning meditation at 6 a.m. He has about 45 minutes before he takes breakfast at 7 a.m. I am meeting him at 6.15 a.m. to brief him on his day. I can give you 15 minutes, between 6.15 a.m. and 6.45 a.m., to speak with him. You owe me a big one. This is a very special favour, you got it?"

Antonio clasped his palms into a prayer gesture and raised them to his lips, "Thank you! Thank you! Thank you! I owe you one big favour!"

ANGER, GREED, AND MINDFULNESS

6 a.m., Hotel Monastery. Old Town Prague
Antonio reached the hotel and could not resist the aroma of coffee. He walked into the cafe to get his first shot of caffeine for the day. This charming hotel used to be a monastery when it was founded in 1140 AD. It was a 20-minute walk from the Charles Bridge, which gave Antonio time to think of the questions he had for Monk Matt.

Theresa showed up at 6.05 a.m. She wore a white blouse, a pink scarf around her neck, and navy blue trousers. Her hair was tied in a bun, and she looked absolutely radiant. She told Antonio to come into the meeting room, situated next to the cafe in exactly 10 minutes.

Monk was seated on a chair behind a table, in a small room with stone concave wall ceiling. It looked like a small prayer room from the early days when this place was a monastery. Theresa sat on the floor, briefing the monk on the day's activities. When Antonio walked in, Monk looked up. He recognised the man immediately and gave him a wide smile. "How are you, Antonio?"

Antonio smiled back. With clasped palms, he gestured with a bow of his head as he approached Monk. Theresa signalled for Antonio to sit in a chair opposite the Monk, across the table. For some strange reason, speaking with Monk Matt in this manner reminded him of the times when he made confessions at the Catholic chapel during his school days.

Monk asked, "Did you attend the talk last evening with your two friends?"

Antonio replied, "Yes, I was at your talk with Toby. But Charles did not attend. He was supposed to join us later, but it seemed that he could not escape from his company's award dinner last night."

Monk nodded. "The busy executive, always having someone's priority to attend to. Did the talk answer some of your questions?"

Antonio reached into his breast pocket for his notes as he answered, "Yes, yes, the talk was very useful. In fact, I have some additional questions I would like to seek your advice on. There were so many people last evening after the talk so I thought it would be better that I speak with you separately. And thanks to Theresa, I was able to arrange for some time this morning."

Monk nodded, "Of course. One of a monk's daily duties is to spread the knowledge of Dhamma, which is the teachings of Buddha. What questions do you have?"

Antonio appreciated Monk's efficiency in getting to the point as he glanced at his watch, hearing Theresa's voice in his head, "Only 15 minutes! Keep it short!"

Antonio went on to ask several questions about anger, emotions, and sense-desires attachment. He also asked for permission to record the conversation on his phone so that he could listen back to it later. Monk agreed, as long as Antonio did not post it on the Internet.

"How do I control my anger and emotions?" asked Antonio. "I get impatient with incompetent people. In my business, we cannot tolerate mistakes. The profit margins are thin. We want to give our customers a great product and a unique quality service experience, yet keep it affordable. That is my differentiator. It's easy to charge a premium for superior goods, but my unique model is to price affordably for top-quality products. In order to do this, my cost control has to be very tight. This means that at the backend, we cannot afford to make mistakes. Every mistake requires ten more sales to recover the loss. I've gotten really angry with some of my kitchen staff who have wasted food. I've fired people who did not meet the customers' requests on time. The product marketing brochure must be perfect, without mistakes. How can I maintain sanity, and not be angry, when everything depends on perfect execution?"

Monk nodded, "That's a good question. What else is bothering you?"

Antonio responded, "This has something to do with the topic of greed. I seem to be caught in an infinite cycle of building new businesses. The more successful I became, the more projects I wanted to create. I get excited by new ideas and concepts. My mind cannot stop looking forward to newer and more greener opportunities. I feel like I am constantly living in the dream of a better future. Each time I accomplish a goal, I start looking for another one to conquer. The thing is, I was happy with what I had gained. But when you asked who would wait for me at the finish line, I could not answer. I am not unhappy now, but neither am I happy. How do I get out of this cycle? I guess this is desire, right?"

"Yes, greed and desires are interrelated," replied Monk. "Greed refers to the acquisition of tangible material things, power, financial wealth, or possessiveness. Desires are caused by the six sensory organs and their associated cravings: the eyes, sight; the ears, sounds; the nose, smells; the tongue, tastes; the skin, touch; and the Mind, thoughts. Monk can explain that in detail later. What other questions do you have?"

Antonio was glad that Monk let him unload all his thoughts before he answered them. This seemed to be a good technique in handling questions, so Antonio made a mental note to use this technique the next time he had to deal with questions at his company meetings. It would give him time to construct the answer while listening to all the questions. It could also offer a broader perspective of all the questions so he could batch the common ones to answer together.

Antonio continued with his next question. "I've heard many definitions of mindfulness. What is it really? And how do I use it to help me be a happier person? And that's my last question, for now."

Monk maintained a smile and seemed to scan his thoughts as his eyeballs rolled upwards slightly. He tilted his head to one side, cocking his ears as if listening to his internal thoughts. Then he looked at Antonio and replied with a calm tone.

"So, your questions are on the topics of anger control, greed, and mindfulness: If we tackle your question on mindfulness first, that will solve your first question on impatience and anger. And when we tackle the second question of greed and the infinite cycle of your business, then you will also understand Desires better."

Antonio squinted his eyes and pouted his lips as if to analyse Monk's point and find an angle to dispute the argument. Then he laughed, "Ha ha ha! You are right! If I stop building more businesses, then I might not even need to worry about business. But how do I survive without money?"

Monk smiled, "How to survive without money... well, that depends on how much you need to stay alive. The last words of Buddha before he left this world into Nirvana were 'be heedful.'"

Antonio furrowed his brow. "What does that mean?"

"Heedful is to be attentive, diligent, or conscientious," explained Monk. "Sometimes it's used as a reference to compare so as to explain mindfulness, although it is not really the same. To be mindful is to be aware of the present, the past, and the future states. It means to be consciously aware that things are changing all the time.

Time never stops. The cells in our body grow and die every second. In fact, an average adult has about fifty billion cells dying a day. This means that the body needs to regenerate fifty billion new cells to replace them. The sun and moon keep revolving. The flame of a candle is different every second. It is never the same flame that is burning. Thus, when we experience something good, we need to be mindful that it won't be in the same state the next time as nothing is permanent. If we get attached to the present state, we might be angry when it is no longer the same. A husband may find a young and beautiful wife with the body of a model. Over time, she won't look the same despite spending lots of money on skincare and body surgery. Will he love her the same? That would depend. As long as we are attached to something and expect it to be unchanged, we will be disappointed — and that causes unhappiness, and that is being un-mindful."

Antonio had a thought. "What if our business was going through a rough patch, and it started to become better as the economy improved. That is positive change for the better and I am not disappointed by that. Not all change is bad, right?"

"Yes," said Monk, "when a bad situation starts to improve, it feels good. When your business was in a rough patch, you did not want it to stay that way. In fact, you would probably do whatever you can to get out of that situation. That was stressful. But once things become better, you want to hold on to it by doing whatever you can to prevent it from declining. In both situations, you were stressed. You are stressed because you want to get out of a bad situation, and you are stressed because you want to keep it in the better situation. When you remove your self-interests, ego, or personal stake from any event, the event stands alone as an unbiased event. Dealing with the changing situation without ego, self-interest, and personal stake is a good approach to practising Mindfulness.

"It's like watching a football match as a bystander, with no vested interest in which team wins or loses. This event is considered as Empty in Buddhism. An Empty event does not affect you. On the other hand, the potential of this Emptiness depends on your mind. If you have a corrupted mind, you could take advantage of it in a selfish way that only benefits you. If you have a generous mind, you could take advantage of it for the betterment of others. Or if you have an equanimous state of mind, you could walk away and not be tempted by this event at all."

"I think I understand," said Antonio. "A year ago, one of my customers was closing his business. He invited me to view a plot of land in Malaysia which he was looking to sell at a discount of 20 per cent below market rate because he needed instant cash. I did not have any need for the land, but I saw an opportunity to buy it cheap and sell it when the market was right. So that situation was an example of a Empty situation. Thereafter, I became greedy and attached to it the idea that I could benefit from his crisis. Even though I did not need it, I was tempted by the commercial opportunity and took a risk. I negotiated for an even lower price at 30 per cent below valuation and felt I had a really good deal. I took the risk that it would not devalue by more than 30 per cent. So, I took a bank loan to pay for this plot of land. Five years later, I am still holding on to this land. The market declined by only 10 per cent but I did not expect the currency to fall in value by 25 per cent. Including my bank interest of 6 per cent per year, I have already lost money on this investment, which I should have just ignored. Sigh!"

Monk nodded, "That's a good example of how Greed played a role in turning an Empty situation, which was neutral, into an undesirable situation for you. Once the person is attached to an event, it is no longer Empty. And once the person has an expectation for it to go up or down, or for foreign exchange rates to be constant, all these actions motivated by excessive greed will lead to suffering.

"So, in summary, being Mindful is to be aware that everything is constantly changing, including our body and mind. To be involved without being attached is the balance we need to achieve a state of Mindfulness. The voice of Greed could whisper to us to hold on to it and wait for the market to improve. The voices of Fear and Anger could tell us to get rid of it. The voice of Delusion could tell us not to worry, be happy, as we could get lucky. On the contrary, to ignore the situation by refusing to know about that situation is not mindfulness. That is being ignorant."

Antonio glanced at the door, hoping that Theresa had forgotten about them so that he could still have more time with Monk. Suddenly, a light bulb seemed to come on inside Antonio. "So, Mindfulness is to be aware that things are impermanent. Everything will change. Humans will age. Material objects will decay. Relationships may deteriorate or improve. Economies will go up or down. Currencies will devalue or improve. Our past events cannot be changed. Our future events are influenced by how we act today. We need to be aware and be mindful that things we enjoy today may not be the same tomorrow. Our past experiences, guilt, anger, happiness, or joy can be changed by creating new responses to these past events. We don't have to be stuck with the old feelings of these past events. Being prepared to let go of the past is Mindfulness. When we create perfect dreams of our future, we are likely to be disappointed if we are not mindful. Being prepared to let go of a fixed expectation of the future is Mindfulness. Things change, and dreams need to adapt. Holding on to a perfect vision of the future will lead to anger and disappointment. Being mindful is to be present and to enjoy what we have, but without being fixated on an expectation. Being mindful is NOT about 'I don't care', or 'ignore it', or 'avoid it'. That's apathy, irresponsibility, and delusion."

Monk smiled and nodded, "That is a perfect understanding of Mindfulness. Now, can you see how that would help you with your first question on being impatient with incompetence and angry with people who fail to live up to your standard?"

Antonio nodded slowly while looking into the distance with a pursed lips and squinted eyes. "Yeees. Yes. I guess I've got to set the right expectation and make it clear to my team what is good and what is tolerable. When they are within the tolerance range, I will be mindful that nothing is absolute. Nobody is exactly the same; otherwise we would just be mechanical artificial intelligence robots. Also, when I sense that things are approaching the limits of the tolerance range, I should probably get involved early when the situation has not reached crisis mode. Otherwise I will be steaming angry and shouting at everyone. I usually get angry because I've gotten involved when it's too late for me to correct it. So, I need to get in early in the game."

Monk queried, "How can you be involved in every one of these situations and get in early? How do you know when it is early enough?"

"I cannot be in every place all the time," said Antonio. "And perhaps I am juggling too many priorities today. I keep starting new businesses just as the last one is about to be profitable. I take the profit from the last one to fund the new investments. So I am perpetually in a cash-tight situation. The goal was for all these investments to be profitable in the long run. They would snowball with increasing momentum and I would be super rich. The reality is, nothing is constant. I expected the businesses to be self-running once I babysat it for a while. And when it started to be profitable, I left them to operate independently. I hired people to manage them and expected my staff to operate and grow the businesses. The reality is that we are dealing with people. And people are different. They have different motivations. Gosh! I wish I could clone myself. Hmm, maybe that's not a bad idea. I should invest in stem-cell cloning! Ha ha, just joking.

"My staff don't work the same hours as I do. I treat every business as my own and give my life to them. But employees are not like me. Even if I gave them shares in the business, I cannot expect them to put work ahead of self or family. I need to change. I need to slow down and I need to be Mindful that things are always changing, and that nobody and nothing is the same. And even if they are the same for a while, they won't remain the same. Also, it would be great if everyone in my team adopted this Mindfulness concept. If I am the only mindful person, then the ball is always in my court to defuse the situations, right? Mindfulness — that's cool!"

Monk then said, "One simple reminder of mindfulness practice daily is to think about breathing. As we breathe in and out, we strive to maintain equanimity and a balanced mind. We remind ourselves that our underlying preference for pleasant feelings often arises from desire, which can lead to greed for sensual pleasure. But when we crave pleasure, we always end up suffering, because like all impermanent things, pleasure eventually changes or disappears. We also remember that our underlying tendency to avoid unpleasant feelings often arises from resentment, which can lead to anger. We observe these tendencies, our greed and our anger, and then let them go, returning our attention to the breath."

Antonio asked, "Would Mindfulness solve my anger management issue completely?"

Monk replied, "It would solve more than half of that. The other part is to practise generosity and loving kindness. The more we spread our love to others unconditionally, the purer our hearts become. It will become easier to be generous and compassion to others. You can practise that with meditation, like what we did at the park. Remember?"

Antonio nodded and made a resolution to learn meditation and be very good at it.

Monk went on, "Anyone can get angry — even the most innocent and pure-minded person. Think of the mind as a pot of clear water, one where you can look straight through the glass pot. When the pot gets heated up, the temperature of the water starts to rise causing tiny bubbles to form, which eventually becomes a pot of bubbling boiling water. You cannot look through the pot anymore because of the boiling water. An angry mind is like a pot of boiling water. Adding heat to the pot is like adding expectations and desires to the mind. The more we add, the more the mind heats up. The bubbles are all the emotions of anger, hatred, sadness, etc. So, keeping the mind cool is like keeping the water cool, by smiling, breathing, meditating, and most importantly, being mindful."

Antonio wrote on his notepad:

Techniques to control anger, hatred, or other negative emotions:

1. Mindfulness. Be aware that things change constantly. Don't get fixated on one expectation.
     Practise: Breathing to calm the mind.
2. Develop compassion and generosity. When the mind is compassionate, it seeks to understand others from their point of view, and not to judge from our point of view.
     Practise: Acts of charity. Sharing loving kindness.
3. Activities that can 'cool the mind': Breathing, smiling, meditating, compassion, love, kindness, awareness
4. Activities that could 'boil the mind': Judgement of others, mismatched expectations, lack of knowledge, assumptions

"Now to your second question," said Monk, "about getting out of the cycle of investing and building bigger businesses. This has to do with contentment. Let me explain about the common misconception of contentment. Contentment is NOT about settling for less. It is NOT about lowering one's standards, downgrading one's lifestyle, being stingy, and not doing anything. It is the opposite of these. Contentment is to be able to improve one's situation to the highest level of one's ability. It's about doing your best. It is about continually improving oneself and one's environment. It is about having the zeal for a better life and improvement. The secret is to do all that without comparing and competing against others and creating discontentment. When one starts to compare, one raises the expectation level that is benchmarked with an external force. That creates discontentment."

Antonio said aloud, "Wait... Let me think. So, being content is to be able to improve your situation to the highest level of your ability, without comparing with others. Okay, okay, I like that. And… and it does not mean abandoning your aspirations, or settling for living with just the basics." Antonio was still reflecting on this new definition when Monk added.

"Some people think that monks are simple-minded and laid-back people. They think that monks don't push themselves and cannot handle stress and do not fit in the real world. They think that monks just want to sit and meditate or chant unintelligible sutras and escape from the world where real progress happens."

Antonio raised his eyebrows. "Yes, isn't that the reason people give up everything to be a monk? So they can relax and do nothing?"

"Yes, a monk's life is simple," explained Monk Matt, "but it is not achieved by doing nothing. The philosophy of Contentment is for one to put one's best effort towards any task or job assigned to them. Every monk at my temple has a job. Monks at my temple are well-educated so their impact on society is more than just doing menial labour work like growing vegetables, or recycling handicraft to sell for a livelihood. For me, I chose to be ordained as a monk because I believed that the world has too much hatred. It is for this reason that my Temple has assigned me the job of spreading the message of Peace through meditation internationally. I have been travelling the world over the past six months, visiting fifty countries, to do just that. The simple message is that Peace begins inside oneself, and through meditation, one can be peaceful inside and hence, affect the world outside. However, we do not compare with others on their peace efforts, nor do we compete against other government or private peace organisations on whose peace efforts are better. We measure ourselves on the number of people we have spread the message to and attended our meditation workshops. Contentment is to set goals and stretch ourselves to achieve what we believe we can and we want to do. We don't use external factors to measure ourselves. For example, we don't measure ourselves with the Happiness Index or Peace Index. Nor do we push our Meditation Centres around the world by imposing Key Performance Indicators or giving them incentives or penalties."

Antonio was puzzled. "How do you make money? How do you fund these efforts?"

"Firstly, we are a non-profit," said Monk, "so, we don't make money through these efforts. These events are funded through donations."

Antonio was impressed with this and had lots of ideas. But he realised that Theresa had entered the room a few minutes earlier and was nervously looking at her watch. She did not want to interrupt them because it seemed that she too was interested in this talk and was engrossed in the topics.

Monk seemed to have noticed Theresa's presence, more as a sign that he should be moving to his next appointment. "Monk hopes that this has given you some information to answer your queries. We cannot discuss everything in a short time. However, Monk can sense that we will meet again one day. As you reflect on these thoughts, Monk knows that you will know what to do."

Antonio frowned, "But how do I know what I don't know?"

"When you meditate more, your mind will get clearer and purer," Monk assured Antonio. "Sometimes when you get those gut feelings or instinctive feelings about something, that is actually your mind sending you signals. A normal person may sense these feelings but not trust them because his mind overrides them with intellectual logic. When you meditate more, your mind will have a better wisdom to know what they mean. Do you know the difference between knowledge and wisdom, Antonio?"

Antonio was very pleased that Monk had addressed him by his name, and he felt very good. "Please enlighten me. Sorry for the pun."

Monk smiled and said, "Knowledge is what you know; wisdom is what you do with your knowledge."

Antonio liked that one liner, so he wrote it down because he loved one liners.

"Finally, here's some parting advice," said Monk. "Monk knows that you have travelled the world and seen many things in your path as an entrepreneur. Our paths of worldly travels cross similar geography, and the people we meet are similar. Perhaps the difference is that you observe things by looking at them, while Monk observes things by looking into them. Similarly, the first place to start to find contentment, peace, and happiness is to start inside of people. Meditation is a great tool. It is easy to learn, but takes a long time to master. Meditation will be a useful tool to help you transform yourself in your journey ahead. May you find your happiness. May your search for wisdom lead you to transform yourself successfully. May you have great health and lead a long life. May you achieve Nirvana, in this lifetime or in other lifetimes."

Antonio thanked the Monk and walked out of the room, engrossed in his own thought. *What shall I do next?* He was oblivious that Theresa was walking beside him until he had reached the main door and looked up to see her holding it for him. "Theresa, can you help me? I want to change my life and I don't know where to start."

6

LIFE'S INVENTORIES

Everyone thinks of changing the world,
but no one thinks of changing himself.

- Leo Tolstoy -

THE CHANGE

Antonio planned to spend the rest of the week visiting
Prague. He engaged Theresa to be his private tour guide.
He even attended the meditation workshop which Monk
Matt conducted for three hundred people in a hall.

One morning, at a sidewalk cafe, as Theresa was
pouring a cup of tea for Antonio, she asked, "You wanted
to start changing yourself, right?"

"Yes."

"Why do you want to change?"

Antonio paused before replying, "Because I don't like some of the stuff I had been doing in the past. I don't like how I judged everyone and everything. I don't like the fact that I get angry and dissatisfied when people do not meet my expectations. I know I am right most of the time because I always do my research and I read a lot. Many people just accept things without verifying the facts. But that's not the point. The point is, what does all this mean? If I die tomorrow, it does not matter if I am right or smart when no one comes to my funeral. Well, I used to think that I didn't care if nobody showed up at my funeral because I was dead anyway. But now, I think I want to leave a good impact on this world and perhaps bring along good merits, so that my life after this would be in a good place."

"But you are already successful in what you do," said Theresa. "What if changing does not improve your situation? Would you still want to change?"

Antonio replied, "Monk Matt made a lot of sense when he said that I am attached to things that trigger my curiosity and sense of adventure. I felt that I did things because they were fun and exhilarating. The higher I climbed, the more dissatisfied I got, and I always needed a higher challenge to keep me excited. I realised it was the pursuit that kept me going, not the attainment of the goal. Thus, I don't get sustained happiness in both the pursuit and the attainment stages of this process. So, why am I doing it? I need to change so that I can enjoy it all the way."

EMPTY YOUR CUP

Theresa shared a story with Antonio. There was a guy who went to see a monk. He asked the monk for help. The monk told him to relax and let go of his judgement. The man said that he had already done that. The monk then asked him to be more open to others' feedback, be compassionate, and forgive others who offended him. The man told the monk that he had already done that. He said that he had been listening to feedback from others and was being as open as he could be. He said that he had tried to help others, and had showed compassion by donating to temples and helping the less fortunate. The monk then asked him to let go of his possessions and live a simple life. The man replied that he had already given up smoking, moved into a smaller house, reduced from five cars to two, and simplified his lifestyle. He only travelled Economy on flights and booked regular rooms at hotels, not suites. Then the monk asked, "What more do you want since you have already done all these?" The man said, "I have tried everything I know, given as much as I can to others, stopped judging, and started helping others compassionately. But I am still not happy. I want happiness."

The Monk replied, "You have to remove the 'I' and the 'want' from that statement. Then you will get Happiness.

The 'I' represents your ego. As long as a person gives importance to the ego and its self-identity, the attention focus will be on embellishing themselves before helping others. The opposite of self is non-self. When you think of others more than yourself, you begin the process of sharing, loving kindness, and generosity. The 'want' represents the desires. We need to give before we receive."

The man was puzzled, so asked: "How can I do that? Please teach me." The monk reached for the teapot and asked the man, "Can I pour you some tea?" The man realised that he had not drunk the tea from his cup, so replied, "My cup is still full. I don't need more tea now. Thank you."

The monk said, "You have just found your answer."

The man looked even more puzzled.

The monk explained, "When your cup is full, you cannot receive more tea from my teapot. You need to empty what you know and what you have learnt before you can receive new knowledge. If one method did not work, we try harder, and use other methods. At some point, it may be necessary to completely empty whatever we knew. Sometimes it is the very knowledge and skills that we possess that are blocking us from learning new things and new ways to do things. Just like your cup of tea.

"The reason you are not able to be happy is because your cup is still full. Whatever you do, you will not be fulfilled because you have not emptied all of the 'I' and the desires from your 'wants.'"

When Theresa finished her tale, Antonio looked into the distance, lost in thought. He knew that the philosophy was true, but it was easier said than done. It was hard to empty his cup when he was in the midst of building his businesses, as everything was interdependent. Yet, he was determined to find a way to escape from this trap.

SORTING OUR PRIORITIES

Theresa, sensing that Antonio was stuck, decided to lighten the mood and broke the silence. "I used to play a game with tourists when we were on a really long boring coach ride. It's called 'Things that Matter Most to Me.'"

Antonio heaved a sigh, relieved to be pulled back from his deep thoughts. "How do you play it and what was the point of the game?"

Theresa explained, "The object of this game is to identify things that are most dear to us. Most people have a lot of stuff they want and may not need, and lots of stuff that they need, but may not want. So, by listing only ten items, they are forced to prioritise. There are usually five categories: Material things I own, Activities I do, Relationships I value, Roles I play, and Values I cherish. Sometimes, we use this exercise as a way to make an inventory of our life. And if we only had a limited time to live, listing things down gives us clarity on what matters to us most. I did this exercise a few years ago with my girlfriend and that was why I decided to be a tour guide;

so that I could see the world, instead of being stuck in the kitchen of my mum's restaurant."

Antonio liked the game and felt that it was appropriate for him, at this stage of his life, to take stock of the things that were most important to him. "This sounds like fun. Sure, let's do that. Here, I have a notepad and pencils."

They made space to write at the table and Antonio started on the first category with gusto.

Possessions that are important to me:
1. Money — financial stability
2. My BMW
3. Computer — cannot live without it. Whole life is in there.
4. Watch collection
5. House
6. My library of books, magazines
7. Gadgets
8. Mobile phone
9. McIntosh Sound System
10. Golf Club memberships

Antonio wrote furiously, then said, "Done!" Theresa had finished as well. "Okay, let's list 'Activities I like to do," she said.

Antonio dived into his list.

Activities I like to do:
1. Travel — love seeing new places
2. Attending conferences — love learning new stuff
3. Racing go-karts — love the speed and adrenaline
4. Thinking of new ideas — love stretching my mind
5. Setting up new businesses — love creating new businesses and see them grow
6. Networking and meeting new people — love to talk and hear different perspectives from others
7. Eating good food — love testing new restaurants and unique dishes
8. Smoking cigars — great to have a good cigar to relax over whisky once a while
9. Drinking good wine — nothing beats the diverse flavour of red wines
10. Solving puzzles — stretching the brain constantly

Antonio finished his list and looked up with a big smile.

Theresa said, "Done! Next..."

"I know," said Antonio. "Let's make a list of relationships that we value and don't want to give up." Theresa nodded, and Antonio wrote on his notepad.

Relationships that are important to me:
1. Mom
2. Sister, Clara
3.

Antonio struggled with this. He was stuck at two, but pushed himself for a few more.

Relationships that are important to me:
1. Mom
2. Sister, Clara
3. Good friend, Raj
4. YPO Forum buddies
5. High School friend, AC
6. ??

Antonio stared at his list for a while but could not think of anyone else to add. He looked up and asked, "Is it ok if I only have five?"

Theresa had noticed him struggling with this category so she had slowed down deliberately. She had more than ten but reduced it to keep within the set parameters. She smiled and realised that it was very easy for her to make friends. Ironically, even though Antonio was so successful, relationships did not come easy for him. "You miserable man," she teased. "Okay, let's move on. Next list is roles we play in our lives. These are roles that we take on or we are born into, like being a daughter or son, and we want to keep playing these roles. They could also include being a father, son, businessman, leader, friend, tour guide, little league football coach, or a business community leader at clubs."

Antonio started writing even before Theresa finished explaining.

My Roles that are important to me:
1. Entrepreneur
2. Son
3. Lecturer of business at a local community college
4. Creator of business start-ups at Angel Investor Club
5. YPO Regional Chairperson
6. Chair Member of local Chamber of Commerce
7. CEO of his group holding company, with ten subsidiaries
8. Regional Chapter chair at Business Network International

"That was a tough list," said Theresa, as Antonio finished his list. "I realised that sometimes I did things for the tour company, like designing new brochures because I am a graphic designer, but I never got recognised for the work not compensated."

"Really? What a cheapo company!" retorted Antonio.

Theresa clarified, "No, no, it's not their fault. I volunteered to gain experience. Anyway, let's move on. Now let's do the last one — Values I cherish. These are the non-measurable principles, beliefs, values, philosophies that we hold dear inside our hearts that guide how we behave and respond to situations externally."

Values that are important to me:
1. Freedom
2. Honesty
3. Impactful
4. Integrity
5. Generosity
6. Kindness
7. Intelligence
8. Fun
9. Humour

When they were both done, Theresa said, "Next, we circle the top three items in each category."

Antonio was confident that he could pick three easily. After 10 minutes, he said, "Here you are. My top three items per list."

Theresa grinned, "Let's hear it!"

Antonio and Theresa shared their lists then discussed the similarities and differences between their priorities. Antonio realised that this simple exercise required a lot of introspection and reflection. He discovered that writing things down forced him to think about everything in his life in order to select the ten most important ones, before narrowing them down to three.

He also noticed that there were things that he spent most of his time on that didn't make it into the top three. *Then why am I spending my time on it?* he asked himself. For instance, he realised that he spent so much time and money collecting rare stamps and old vinyl records; yet these two did not even make it to his top ten list. He had an entire room of these records that he had bought over the years. But what was he going to do about them? His turntable and sound system cost him hundreds of thousands of dollars, but he hardly had time to listen to them.

Theresa realised that her collection of designer handbags and scarfs were more than what a regular person should own. Having a whole closet of over a hundred and fifty scarfs was insane. She collected branded scarfs from Hermès to handmade Pashmina ones from India. Her expensive handbag collection was her pride and joy. Her cheapest Prada bag cost more than $1,500. Yet, none of these made it to the top three items of her possessions list. What did make it were her father's Seiko watch, her Girl Guide scarf, and the bracelet her mum had given her for her twenty-first birthday.

Antonio said, "I remember Monk said that when a person leaves this world, he does not bring anything with him except his karma and his habits. So, all these items that we listed are only significant to us when we are alive?"

Theresa nodded, "Yes. Do you remember that story from Monk about the man with four wives?"

Antonio admitted, "Not really. I must have dozed off or was distracted or something. Can monks have wives?"

Theresa shook her head. "No, that's not the story. It's a story of a wealthy and good-looking man who had four wives."

"I don't even know if I can handle one wife. This man must be a very capable or a very dumb person." Antonio laughed at his own joke. Theresa did not look amused. She did not like demeaning jokes about women, especially if they were told by men.

Sensing trouble brewing, Antonio apologised, "Ahem, sorry about that. Please tell me that story."

Theresa breathed to relax and calm herself, then proceeded to relate the story that Monk Matt had told the audience during the talk the previous evening.

THE MAN AND HIS FOUR WIVES

Once there was a man who had four wives. He loved the fourth wife very dearly and lived with her and spent lots of time with her. He would get her the most stylish dresses and exquisite jewellery, and entertained with her all the time. She loved him, and he loved her.

He also loved his third wife. He visited her weekly and he would give her everything she wanted. She was the one who controlled everything in his life.

The man's second wife was also his confidante. He visited her once a month and she was the one to whom he would tell all his personal matters to. He could always talk to his second wife about life and such.

His first wife was very capable and independent. He wasn't too attached to her. He would visit her once every six months. She was modest, always trying her best to show herself. But the man did not give a lot of attention to her.

One day, the man was told by his physician that he had contracted a rare form of leukaemia, a cancer of the blood. He only had a month to live at most. There was no cure for his illness and he was advised to prepare himself for the final day. The man was very shocked and sad. He could not believe that this was happening to him. He had done many good things and felt he did not deserve this.

In his depressive state, he called his fourth wife to seek consolation. After hearing the bad news, the fourth wife realised that that the man would not be useful to her anymore. She wished him good luck and told him that she would leave him the moment he breathed his last. She showed no emotion or feeling, and started to pack her things. The man's heart was broken. After giving her all his attention and wealth, she was heartless and showed no sympathy for him in his moment of need.

The man went to visit his third wife and told her about his condition. The third wife consoled him but then told him that she would need to find someone else she could be with since he would not be around for too long. She asked for his approval to be with someone else. The man was devastated by the practicality of his third wife.

He then called his second wife, hoping to get some sympathy. The second wife told him that she would support him till his final moments and give him a good sending off. The man felt more consoled and cried with guilt that he should have treated his second wife better and spent more time with her.

Finally, he felt compelled to inform his first wife about his condition. The first wife, upon hearing the news, calmly told the man, "I will support you all the way and through your final days, and beyond. I will die and go with you to wherever you go after your death." The man cried as he did not deserve this from the wife whom he took for granted and spent the least amount of time with.

Theresa stopped.

Antonio, jaw slightly opened, frowned and said. "So? What does this mean? It's only a story, right?"

Theresa said, "Monk Matt went on to explain the moral of this story. In the story, the fourth wife represents our body and our cravings, which we give so much effort and time to, only to leave it behind when we die. The third wife represents our hard-earned wealth, money, material possessions, and properties, which will belong to others after we die. The second wife represents all the friends and family who can only comfort us and accompany us as far as the grave. The first wife represents the Mind or Soul, which has always been there for us but receives the least amount of attention from us when we are alive. Our Mind/Soul is the only part that follows us to our next journey, yet we often realise its devotion only at the end of our lives."

Theresa stopped and looked at Antonio, "So, that's the story of the man and his four wives."

THE TRIPLE GEMS

Antonio had his right elbow at the edge of the coffee table, his chin and cheek resting on his palm. The fingers of his left hand were twiddling a pencil vigorously. This was one of his habits when he was engaged in deep thought. He needed something in his hands while his brain cranked out new ideas. Years ago, Antonio was a chain-smoker and holding a cigarette was the most natural thing to do while he thought. Since the death of his business partner from lung cancer, Antonio made a resolution at his funeral to quit smoking. He threw away his pack and never touched a stick again. That was ten years ago. His determination was so strong that whatever he put his mind to usually got done.

Out of the blue, Antonio said, "I've got an idea!" and without waiting for Theresa to respond, he continued, "Let's push ourselves further. Let's take the lists we have created and pick only three items from all the five categories. These three items are the only ones that we will keep till the last moments of our life. Learning from the story of the man and his four wives, if he had thirty days to live, he would have to reduce his priorities to only the most important and significant ones that he had time to focus on. So, as we approach our final days, what would be the three things that we will keep with us to our deathbed?"

Antonio turned towards Theresa, his eyes narrowed into a piercing look. Theresa was biting her lip as she looked at her list. Already she was realising that having a long list of items made it even harder to select only three. At first, she was pleased with herself for having a full list for all the five categories. Now she realised that having more was not necessarily a good thing. "Umm... Okay, that's a good idea. I need time to look through my lists. I think I may have too many items here."

Antonio smiled, "It's about lunchtime now. Let's order some food. While waiting for our order, we can reflect on our lists. We should not rush through this. This is an important step."

Looking through the restaurant menu was a relief for the brain after what they just went through working on the lists. Once they ordered, each went back to scrutinising their lists. From afar, they looked like a couple sitting together but not speaking to each other. They studied some documents separately, occasionally looking into the distance before glancing down again and thinking hard. Their lips moved as if they were speaking to themselves, and they chewed on the ends of their pencils as if making some tough choices. Then they would mark a paper with the pencil before moving on to another sheet and staring into the distance again.

Antonio worked through his lists diligently. He had

a method of selecting and prioritising things like this, and he used it to make tough choices, weighing the pros and cons of each item. For the first step, he took time to scan through his list and, using his gut feel, he picked his top three items from the list of all five categories. Then for the second step, he would pit each of the remaining items ('the challenger') against each of the top three items (the 'contender') which he had picked in step one. If the 'challenger' item was more important than the 'contender' item, then the challenger would bump the contender down one position, while the challenger took its place in the top three.

Antonio looked through his lists and picked what he felt were the most important: Teacher (from the Roles list), Spiritual Self (also from the Roles list), and Money (from the Things list). That was step one. For step two, he picked Freedom (from the Values list) as the challenger and pit this against the three items he had chosen. The question he asked himself, as a litmus test, was: *If today were the last day of my life, would this item X be what I will hold on to? Would it be more important than item Y till the last minute of my life?*

Unfortunately, Antonio did not think that Freedom was more important, so he struck it off his list. He then chose Generosity (also from the Values list) and had this challenge his top three selections again. Antonio felt that Generosity ranked as more important than Money, but less important than Spiritual Self. So, he swopped out Money for Generosity and the latter became one of the items on the top three list. Antonio then repeated this process laboriously until all items on his list had been challenged. What was left would be the top three items representing the top priority items that he wanted to keep. By the end, this was the final list he wrote on his notepad:

1. Activities: Coach others/teach others.
    Impart and transfer my skills and knowledge to help others be successful.
2. Values: Generosity.
    To nurture a generous mind and give to charity and communities in need of help.
3. Role: Spiritual Self.
    To develop my spiritual self.

Antonio loved visual representations. It helped him to remember better. So, he drew a circle to represent his selections.

Once he made his choices and wrote them down, he felt a heavy burden lifted from him. He was very pleased with his selection. This process made him realise

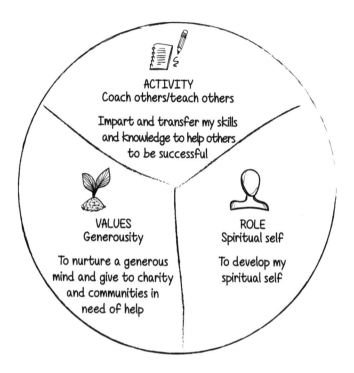

ACTIVITY
Coach others/teach others

Impart and transfer my skills
and knowledge to help others
to be successful

VALUES
Generousity

To nurture a generous
mind and give to charity
and communities in
need of help

ROLE
Spiritual self

To develop my
spiritual self

that his emptiness was caused by his focus on building businesses and adding adventures to his life's bucket list. His first priority of being a teacher and coach would satisfy his intellectual quest because he wanted to share his knowledge and wisdom as gifts to others. His gifts to others were the lessons from his own business adventures. The purpose was to teach others the How's, inspire them with the Why's, and achieve the What's of success.

The value of generosity, his second priority, would allow him to channel his purpose and energy into distributing instead of accumulating. Greed and attachment would not lead to happiness. In fact, they led in the opposite path, away from happiness.

The third priority of developing his own spiritual self would be a step to eliminating the Ego-mind from his consciousness. He acknowledged that this was his weakest asset and that his 'spiritual bucket' was mostly empty. This was where he needed put in a lot of work and focus on developing his Mind.

The story of the man and his four wives reminded him that his body and wealth were material things and relationships were impermanent, and that they would all disappear when he left this world. Only his Mind or Soul would move on to the next existence. He knew that he needed to spend time with that 'first wife', to develop his Mind/Soul so that when it went to the next existence, he would have a better chance of going to heaven.

The question of where the soul went after leaving the body was less of a concern to Antonio. All he knew now was that he needed to spend more effort in developing his Mind and Soul. Where the Mind or Soul went to after a person died would be different, depending on what religion a person believed in. Antonio remembered reading from Catholic school that a person's soul could go to a place called Purgatory after a person died. His current Christian church's Pastor explained that there is eternal life with God after death. Monk Matt mentioned that after this lifetime, a person's mind would go into another existence in different realms, through a process call Rebirth.

Antonio felt that, regardless of whether a person went to church or temple, whether they engaged in prayers or meditation, there existed a mighty force or energy that governed the universe. Some call it God; some call it Karma; some call it Science; others call it Logic. What had not been or could not be proven did not mean that it did not exist. Antonio remembered Theresa's argument that gravity existed even before Newton was able to prove it scientifically and put a formula to it. Antonio now believed that the truth was: There is 'life' after death. It existed whether one chose to believe it or not. Believing in something was an Ego-driven mentality because 'I' was the judge of that decision. Whether 'I' believed it or not was the choice of how 'I' wanted to see the reality based on 'I''s version of the truth. Antonio started to rationalise that after we die, our Mind/Soul would leave our body. The Mind/Soul would either go to heaven, to hell, or to somewhere in between. The existence of the Mind/Soul in any of these places could either be referred to as Rebirth, Reincarnation, or Eternal life. These were just given different terms by different religions or theological studies. Either way, Antonio reasoned that there was an afterlife beyond death. So, he needed to invest in his spiritual development of the Mind and Soul so that he could move to the next place with a better start.

The waiter came with their food. Theresa had ordered a Greek salad and a cheese pizza while Antonio had asked for the popular Prague dish of braised duck with mandarin orange sauce. The smell of the food made him hungry. He looked out of the window towards the river and his mind drifted away to imagine how his life would be when he started implementing his three new priorities. He decided to give it a name. He called them his Triple Gems: Coach/Teacher, Generosity, and Spiritual Self.

7

FIVE MONTHS LATER

Quiet people have the loudest minds.
- Stephen Hawkings -

CAUGHT IN THE WHEEL

January was the Mid-Year Review period in M-Reality's business cycle. It had been five months since the Worldwide Sales Meeting in Prague. Budgets had been set then in July, at the beginning of the financial year, and January was the mid-point of execution in the full year's plan. Thus, it was called the Mid-Year Review, or MYR for short. While most companies reviewed their business quarterly, M-Reality used the mid-point to review all the microscopic details of the execution plans. They would review all lessons learnt from mistakes made in the First Half of the financial year, and recalibrate the plans and projection for the Second Half. This was a good practice, which allowed the company to stay ahead of the competition and be so successful all these years. However, because of the intensity of these reviews and the political jostling for resources, most employees did not look forward to it. Which was the reason why MYR was nicknamed 'Mind Your Rear'.

Charles's business division had undergone a difficult First Half. Most of the Asian economies were affected by the currency depreciation and economic impact from the US financial credit crisis. His team was 10 per cent down on the sales target, which meant that MYR would be a very tough discussion for them. Fortunately, he had been quick to act on his austerity drive to reduce costs, so his profitability was on track. In the run-up to the review, Charles had to go through the performance reports from his teams for eleven countries and compare the actual performance with the budgeted targets. As he pulled out his notes from the Worldwide Sales Meeting, a piece of paper fell out from the pile. On it were his reflections after the meeting with the Monk. Even though Charles was too busy to be bothered by anything other than matters related to MYR, he decided to glance at the note:

Today is the first day of a new life:
To be Successful and Happy

Actions

1. Project Mettā   Call Mum. Tell her I love her.
                         Date: Next week
2. Project Mettā   Call Amy. Tell her the things I
                         appreciate about her.
                         Date: Next week
3. Project Compassion   Check on Toby. He is in a difficult
                         situation. Maybe I can help.
                         Date: Tomorrow
4. Project Meditate   Check for classes in Singapore.
                         Date: Start soon
5. Project Simplify   To reduce old stuff I don't need.
                         Give away or have a garage sale till
                         I get rid of all extras.
                         Date: Start next month
6. To quit my corporate job. Retire from M-Reality by 31 Dec,
    three years from today

He closed his eyes and stretched his arms behind
his head. He realised that he had jumped back into the
hamster wheel right after the Prague meeting, albeit a
larger wheel this time, but nevertheless performing the
same motions. His routine was the same as before. He had
called his mum the week after he returned from Prague
and even managed to fly out for a surprise lunch date. She

talked a lot to him then and he had not realised how well she had settled into a new routine after retirement. While his mother kept herself busy with knitting, cooking and distributing food to the homeless community, she was constantly worried about the grandchildren as she did not get to see them anymore. He promised his mum that he would call her weekly to chat and plan a family trip to Osaka to visit her in July during the school holidays.

He and Amy had a great romantic dinner a week after he returned from Prague. He bought several Bohemian crystals for her and for her mother. Amy was delighted. They had a great conversation and cleared up a number of issues between them. He revealed to her his intention to retire in about three years' time and that he would have to figure out a plan to move out of the corporate path. Amy was very supportive and pledged to be ready to downsize their lifestyle to support this plan. She liked to see Charles doing what made him happy rather than what made him wealthy.

Besides these two actions, nothing had really changed and he had not followed through on his other 'projects'.

Charles sighed. *How did I let this happen? I am back on the same wheel as before. Sigh! I have a week to finish my preparation for the final MYR panel. Then I will either get fired, or quit, or have to suffer by working harder for the second half of the fiscal year to recover and make up for the shortfall in sales. All these choices are looking equally unattractive.*

He closed his eyes and breathed deeply again. He only had three hours of sleep the night before due to the conference calls with the US all through the night. His mind drifted as he breathed slowly. Charles remembered how the Monk had led them into a meditation session by getting them to focus inside the body while breathing rhythmically. As he continued to do that, Charles's body started to relax, his mind started to slow down, and he started to sit upright. He felt so serene and relaxed that he lost track of time. Suddenly, an idea popped into his mind and stirred him out of meditation: *I wonder how Antonio is doing.*

Charles picked up his phone instinctively and sent Antonio a WhatsApp message. 'Hey Antonio. How r things going? My business is in deep deep Kimchi and I hv to defend my numbers in a few days with my board. Hope things are better for you in HK.'

Charles and Antonio had continued to communicate on WhatsApp chat for a while since leaving Prague. Charles never made it to the talk by Monk Matt that evening. His company dinner had started late, and after giving out the awards, there was so much celebration and drinking that he never left the place till midnight. The next morning, Antonio had met him for breakfast and given him an update on the talk. Toby had recorded and shared it on his private YouTube channel. However, Charles was having a headache from the hangover and never watched it. Charles realised that Antonio and he were both in the same boat: caught in the infinite cyclical pursuit of happiness and success. They both realised that while they had been successful in business and they were in control of their grand plans, Monk Matt had showed them that they didn't really have full control of their Minds. Their Minds were controlling their beliefs, their values, their philosophies, and their behaviours, and they would live every day in a delusion that they were in control. They really did not have control of their 'monkey mind' and hence did not have control of their lives at all! They both had this belief: 'After all this hard work is done, we will retire and enjoy life.' That delusion led them to work harder and never know when to retire, or how to enjoy their lives after retirement. This is a symptom that affects almost every corporate and business career-driven person.

During breakfast, Antonio had shared with Charles what Monk Matt had said about Greed and Delusion during the previous evening's talk. "You know how much money you have in your wallet now. And probably know how much you have in your bank account. Hence you would spend the money to buy things you want and leave some money for the future and not overdraw the account. So, if time is the currency of your life, would you know how much time you have to live before you die? No, you don't. So how can you say that you will spend your time now to do the things you want, and leave some time for retirement? If you don't know how long your lifespan is, how do you know how close you are to an empty balance of your time on earth? It is a delusion to think that you have balance time 'saved' for retirement and can enjoy the balance of your life.

"This place we call earth is actually a large prison, and we are prisoners on a death sentence. The problem with this prison is that it's so large and unrestrictive that we feel we can do anything we like and go anywhere we want, and there are no bars to restrict us inside our cells. It does not feel like a prison. So we stay in this prison, thinking that we can control our lives. In reality, we do not know when our death sentence will be carried out as our execution date was never told to us. Believing that we can control our lives and that we can have more time later in life to do what we love is a delusion that affects many people. How we live this life is important, how we prepare to leave this life is equally important."

After breakfast, Antonio and Charles made a pledge to find their own solutions to escape from this prison. They both promised to check in with each other on the progress of their own commitments to change and live their lives better. *Beep! Beep! Beep!* Charles's phone alerted him to an incoming message.

Antonio had recognised the American slang 'in deep Kimchi' — which simply meant 'in deep trouble' or more crudely, 'in deep shit'— and knew that Charles must be going through a really tough time. He messaged back: 'Hey Mr Big Guy! Am in Phuket sipping a soda on the beach. Relaxing, man! Sorry to hear about your Kimchi situa. Wanna talk now?'

Charles replied: 'Don't want to spoil your vacation. But yes, talking would be a great relief for my state of mind now. Let me call you.'

The two then chatted for an hour about the economy and the difficult situation with the market. Antonio told Charles that he had already sold off half of his investments. He had taken the chance encounter with Monk Matt at the park in Prague as a message from above. It catalysed his thought process and sparked a chain reaction ahead. The evening talk was the tipping point that gave Antonio the purpose to change his ways. He became less angry in the days that followed due to his daily meditation practices. And instead of worrying about the future and working on new ideas all the time, Antonio focused on enjoying the present and spending time with his family.

Antonio added, "Oh, by the way, Theresa and I are engaged to be married. We don't have a date for the wedding yet, but it should be sometime this year. Man! I am so happy with less things. I found a way to appreciate the things around me which I had taken for granted before. I learnt to love and Theresa has been a blessing. She is so kind and compassionate. Also, I used to get hung up on discussions on which religious practices were the right path. Over the last five months, once I opened up my mind, I started doing research about what Monk Matt said and I realised that, regardless of whether you are Christian, Buddhist, or any other religion, meditation is neutral. It's good for the mind and the soul. I know it worked for me."

Charles was almost envious of Antonio's change. Then he recalled Monk's message not to be jealous or envious of others. Joy comes from rejoicing at others' successes. He remembered specifically Monk's words: "Jealousy and envy are like anger and hatred. They lead one away from a clear mind that sees happiness and defile one's mind with darkness, to see only suffering."

Charles replied, "Hey Antonio, I am so happy for you! The short encounter with Monk Matt in Prague also left a deep impression on me. I wrote down my plans to change, but I hardly did anything with those plans!"

"But you actually made them! And you still have those plans, right?" asked Antonio. "That's a start. Don't beat yourself up. That is life. We get caught up with being busy. Once you get out of the cycle, things get clearer. It's just a slight delay in execution. It's never too late. Make it happen, man!"

Charles was impressed with Antonio positiveness. He thought that Antonio would have beaten him up with his quick one-liners like, 'Fail to plan, and Plan to fail' Or 'A plan without action is a dream without reality'. Instead, with his new attitude, Antonio was being really encouraging and supportive. Charles appreciated Antonio for not kicking him in the ribs when he was down and hurt.

Charles thought to himself: *That's a new Antonio. Wow, something inside this aggressive, fast-talking entrepreneur has changed. He is quite likeable.*

Just then, Antonio said, "Hey Charles, I've got to go. Theresa and I are going to the temple tomorrow morning. I heard that Monk Matt is back in Bangkok. We are trying to meet him to get a shot of new wisdom about planning a family. Look Charles, good luck with your presentation. You will make it through; managing tough situations is your forte. Equanimity is the word, man. Be calm in the midst of all the uncertainty: that's Equanimity."

Charles smiled and regained some self confidence. "Hey Antonio, thanks! Equanimity... yup, good advice. Keeping calm when everything else is in a chaos. That's exactly the advice I needed. Thanks!"

"Oh, one more thing," said Antonio. "Theresa and I are coming through Singapore at the end of the week. You wanna catch up for lunch on Saturday?"

Charles checked his diary and saw that it was completely full. Yet he replied, "Sure! I will shift things around. Let's say 1 p.m. at the Raffles Hotel?"

MID-YEAR REVIEW

MYR was the most stressful period of the year for Charles. After the phone call with Antonio, he was recharged. He knew that while he could address the stress of his business, he was disappointed with himself for losing control of his personal life. Since Prague, he had not focused on his personal commitments. These commitments were so simple to do, but simple things were also easy not to do. It was easier to justify not doing small tasks, even though it was so easy to get small tasks completed. It was not the complexity of the tasks that determined if it would get done. It was the discipline that determined if a person would complete a simple task. For example, doing exercises every morning was a simple commitment, yet it was easier to sleep longer and skip the exercise. Why? Because people tell themselves that they can exercise longer over the weekend to make up for it, and they would be less tired during the week. When tasks are performed repeatedly and consistently, they become habits. Brushing one's teeth when one wakes up and before one sleeps are good habits. Habits make doing things easy. Charles wanted to get through this stressful week before he tackled his personal commitments.

Charles spent the entire week focusing on internal meetings. This was the time of the year where his attention was turned inwards and he avoided any distractions by skipping all customer and partner meetings. This was a legacy work culture passed down from the founder, and had made the company successful. The management belief was "If we don't know our business, we don't own our business. We need to know our market, our customers, and our competition, or somebody else will take it from us."

During the week, Charles drilled the details of team's plans into his staff, to prepare them to tackle any angle of questioning they might receive from the review panel sent to inspect the business. Charles had done this for fifteen years. He had sat at all ends of the table. As a Financial Business Analyst, he was a 'data-cruncher' who created Excel spreadsheets and analysis reports to support the business case. As a Technical Support Manager, he had had to justify the purchase of software and hardware as investments in Information Technology to improve the efficiency and productivity for the team. When he was a Marketing Director, he spent marketing funds to design market programmes that created consumer demands with Pull and Push strategies to drive sales and increase market share. As a business leader, he dealt with everything that the entire subsidiary needed to operate. This included employee satisfaction, customer satisfaction, sales and profits, partner incentive programmes, marketing programmes, consulting and product support services, and government relationships. With his experience, he could be very thorough in helping his team 'scrub through their plans', a term used in the company to represent the scrubbing of dirt and untidiness in a plan. MYR was a very thorough process. There was an internal joke that MYR was as painful as going to the dentist for a root canal operation; painful but necessary.

Friday was the final MYR presentation to the board. Charles's team sat on one side of the U-shaped tables while the review team sat on the opposite side. At the corners were the note takers and observers. Just before it started, Charles engaged the executives and regional managers, all who were part of the review board, in small talk. It is important to build the social connectedness before the formal review.

The MYR turned out to be a nightmare. It was scheduled for Friday from 3 p.m. to 6 p.m., but it went on long and lasted till midnight. There were so many questions and explanations for every single dollar to be spent that it felt like pulling a molar tooth without pain killers. Throughout the entire session, his team was bombarded with so many questions that it felt like a police interrogation. But that's the way this company had been — paranoid about failure and success; but the level of analysis had made them successful and competitive. Charles had been doing this for a very long time, and he knew the drill. Yet each time, it still felt ridiculous. He could not help himself thinking: *MYR really feels like My Year of Regrets.*

Charles remembered Antonio's advice — Equanimity. He maintained a calm composure and was able to manage and deflect all the arrows shot his way. His team was grateful for his leadership and graciousness to take several hits for their misexecutions. Over the years, Charles had built up his emotional bank account, whose credit balance had been built up with the merit points earned from the good deeds done for others in his long corporate career. Now, these credits bought him some sympathy points to shield his team for some of the poor results. Unfortunately, Charles probably used up his entire credit balance in this review.

TEAMWORK: INCH BY INCH, PLAY BY PLAY

Friday, 12.34 a.m., The MYR debrief
Shortly after midnight, the review ended. The room looked like a mess. Papers were strewn all over the floor. The whiteboard was full of writings and diagrams used to illustrate extended discussions. Computer wires and cables were all over the desk. Eventually the team adjourned to the next room which was reserved as their preparation room. They assembled in the room prepared for a debrief session by Charles.

During the debrief, Charles allowed the team to vent a bit about the review. Some went below the belt and blamed others, saying they should have been more accurate with their facts. There was some finger-pointing about who should have done what. Some claimed confusion and even provided email evidence to cover their tracks. A few new members just kept quiet, thinking that they had joined the wrong company. Overall, everyone was very depressed with the outcome. After spending the entire month preparing for this review, they felt demoralised by the interrogation and lack of appreciation of the economic condition that they were up against. The review team tore apart their Business Recovery Plans, as well as challenged every data and analysis of the competition. Their proposed plan that required some investment to expand their markets was shot down and rejected.

Charles knew how these review processes went. It felt like a hurricane had torn through the town. The aftermath was painful, but they needed to pick themselves up and rebuild the town. Fortunately, Charles's team had a few seasoned managers who were able to console the newer members. Overall, Charles needed to give them a pep talk and help the team move forwards. So, he summarised the learning points and gave the talk which he had given many times before. Using an American football metaphor, he called the talk, 'Inch by Inch, Play by Play'. Charles loved telling stories and this one was adapted from one of his favourite movies, *Any Given Sunday*, a 1999 American sports drama film directed by Oliver Stone.

Charles started by asking, "When we are down, when the scores are against us, when you are tired, and up against a formidable enemy, where do you look for strength?"

Everyone looked down and was quiet.

Charles looked around the room. "Where do we find the strength to pick ourselves up and play the game? Not just to play the game to finish, but to play the game to win. I know we are beaten. I know we are tired. I am part of you too. But we still have six months to rebuild these sales and the marketing programmes."

Jane, the marketing executive, retorted, "With no additional marketing dollars, it's like chopping off my left hand after losing my right one!"

Terry, the HR Manager, lamented, "With a headcount freeze, how do we hire the sales team to bring in more sales for the second half?"

"Look team," said Charles, "after the tsunami hit Asia, the town of Phuket in Thailand was devastated. I was there with my family when that happened. Fortunately, that morning, we were up early to tour the northern part of Phuket and were not affected. But when we went back to our hotel, it was a mess! No one could imagine, at that moment, where to start to rebuild Phuket and attract the tourists back. Within a year, the town was rebuilt, and the tourists returned. When you look at Phuket today, it is buzzing as before; as if the tsunami never hit Phuket."

Everyone started to nod and heave deep sighs of relief that they were not affected.

Charles continued, "In American football, the way to score is to keep pushing the line of attack to the goal area. They need to get close enough to score a touchdown or a goal kick. When I was the assistant coach to a high school team, our team was at the final match, and we were losing. During half-time, in the locker room, everyone was beat. They faced a stronger team and could not advance past half field. So, I told them to push forward one inch at a time. Keep pushing forward. Everyone just gains one inch. Every inch is an opportunity. Don't just look for the wide opening or the ten-yard run. Just find that one-inch gap and push. One inch at a time. When

FIVE MONTHS LATER **157**

each of you gains an inch, it adds up to be a yard. Inch by inch, yard by yard.

"And everyone in this team has the accountability to do that. If you are in Sales, you are accountable not only for sales but also to keep costs down to achieve our profitability target. Don't give too much discount. Discounts increase our cost of sales and reduces net profits.

"For Finance folks, your work affects sales too. By approving the sales requests and processing the sales orders faster, we can lock in the sales early to make it for the quarter-ending cycle. Every order counts.

"For HR, we may not have the headcount for this half, but we have a few underperformers we need to move out. Start hiring replacements now, and don't wait for those to leave before recruiting. In this way, we don't lose selling time. The overlap will have minimal cost impact. Everyone has got to look for that extra inch to push forward."

Everyone was now nodding more vigorously. And their heads were being held up, instead of hanging down.

"Team, we have done it before," assured Charles, "and we will do it again. If you disagree with the criticism from the Regional HQ team, prove them wrong! Don't just fight them and disagree with them. Those discussions are over. Now it's time to act and prove to ourselves that we are a team, we are a high-performing team. We can make it and we WILL make it!"

Charles paused to sense the room. He also wanted to use the silence to create the impact of his final punch line.

"Now repeat after me: Inch by Inch, Yard by Yard. Push. Push. Push!"

The team repeated it like a choir singing out of synchronisation: "Inch by inch, yard by yard. Push, push, push!"

Charles, raising his energy, rallied the group. "Come on, team! Say it with conviction! Together, again!" This time the team stood up and in unison repeated loudly, "Inch by inch, yard by yard. Push push push!"

Charles smiled. "I don't know about you all but I never give up. I love sports. Whether it is boxer Manny Pacquiao punching above his weight category to win, or a marathoner agonising a muscle pull on his hamstring to complete the race, it is the WILL that takes a person to the finish line. It is not only the Skills. We can build skills. But for this second half, we must have the WILL to exceed our plans and prove them wrong. The best proof that you are right, is to show the results. Prove we are a team who cares and wins together. What do you think? Can we make it?"

The entire team looked at each other, gritted their teeth, punched their hands in the air, and shouted, "Yes, We Will! Inch by inch, yard by yard. Push push push!"

At that moment, Ted popped his head into the room. Seeing the energy of the team, he smiled and told the team, "I know you will. You all are a great team with a seasoned leader. I know you will! Just let me know what support you need to make it work, okay?"

The team, now even more motivated with this encouragement, nodded back at Ted.

"Charles, I am flying back to Seattle tomorrow on the late red-eye flight," said Ted. "Can we meet at 4 p.m. to finalise all the requests and budgets?"

Charles gave him a hand salute and replied, "Sure Ted. Raffles Hotel at 4 p.m. tomorrow!"

REUNION

Charles slept in till 10 a.m. He woke up drenched in perspiration, then frantically groped for his phone next to the bed. "Oh my gosh! What time is it!" he mumbled. He panicked, thinking that he had missed the MYR meeting. After a few seconds he recovered and realised that this was one of those anxiety moments that haunted him every now and then. He sat up on his bed with his eyes closed and took a few deep breaths. He noticed the smell of fresh coffee and the sweet fragrance of croissant. Amy and the kids had made breakfast for him and left it on a small bedside tray. There was a stalk of flower, a thermos jug with hot coffee, a glass of orange juice, and a few croissants in a basket wrapped inside a white towel. Amy and the kids had gone for a soccer game in school and left him a note to meet them for dinner at Amy's mother's place that night. *Nice touch,* he thought. *It's nice to be home.* His phone alerted him that he had an appointment for lunch with Antonio and Theresa at the Raffles Hotel. He was looking forward to it.

Raffles Hotel, Singapore

Charles was relaxed in his denim jeans and black collarless T-shirt that afternoon. He sat at a corner table at the Empire Cafe in the majestic Raffles Hotel. This is one of the oldest hotels in Singapore, and one of the few 19th century hotels left in the world. Charles liked to bring foreign visitors from Western countries here, and they were often intrigued to learn that the cocktail, Singapore Sling, was concocted in this hotel during the colonial days.

As he was reading the newspapers, a pair of hands covered his eyes from behind. Charles smelt the fragrance of a woman's perfume. Playfully, he reached to pry the hands from his face and felt the smooth and gentle texture of the hands. He then heard a familiar voice, "Guess who?"

Acting surprised, Charles said, "Oh my God! Theresa!"

Charles stood up and turned around to see the beautiful Theresa, wearing a floral blouse with a large straw hat, smiling broadly. They hugged and laughed. Antonio was in a simple white round collared T-shirt, which looked like an Egyptian cotton fabric. Charles loved white cotton fabric. They shook hands and Charles pulled Antonio's shoulder towards him for a man-to-man macho hug.

Charles exclaimed, "Oh my gosh, you guys are a sight for sore eyes! It amazing that you all showed up when I needed you!"

They sat down and started talking non-stop like old friends at a high school reunion. Charles listened to all the amazing updates and changes to their lives after Prague.

Theresa started by raising her left palm and saying, "Here is my happiness." On her fourth finger was a sparkling diamond ring. "After that evening talk by Monk Matt, which you never showed up for, Charles..." She glared in mock anger at Charles, pointing her finger at him. "We need to know your story later. But after that talk, Antonio and I met the next morning and we had a good time together. We realised that we needed to reset our lives."

Antonio jumped in, "We basically pressed the 'Control-Alt-Delete' keys to reboot our lives! We came up with a system to prioritise our lives by taking an inventory of things that matter most to us. After a day of brainstorming, I realised how to fill the emptiness in my life. We called this system 'My Life's Inventory' exercise. Theresa is going to document it so we can run workshops to teach others how to do it.

"I also realised how efficient she was and wanted her to help me sort out my priorities. At first, I asked her to be my personal tour guide. Later, I realised that it was just my excuse to see her again. Maybe the Prague atmosphere added to the romantic mood. We spent the rest of the week together and I proposed to her at the end of that week."

Theresa smiled, "Even though I felt very good about Antonio, I did not want it to be just an impulsive decision.

I've had bad relationships before and did not want to be a victim of another one again. So, I asked Antonio to use time and distance as a test of our true feelings. We dated over the next few months, on Skype, WhatsApp, and short trips together. We visited Venice, Bali, Bangkok, Phuket, KL, and now we are in Singapore. It was just last week in Bangkok that I accepted his proposal!"

Charles was speechless. He is envious of them. He is thinking about his own marriage and wished that he could be in the same state of mind with his family. But he was so busy that there was no room for any personal thinking. "You guys have got to share that life inventory exercise with me. I really need to Control-Alt-Delete my life."

Theresa grinned, "Sure! But do you have time for us, Mr. Busy?"

"Oops, talk about the time," said Charles, "I only have one hour with you guys. I am expected to meet a co-worker at the Long Bar upstairs."

Antonio's eyes widened in mock indignation, "What! A business meeting on a Saturday?"

Charles shrugged, "Ya. Just meeting my boss to finalise the budget numbers. We just had a nightmare of a review yesterday, which lasted till midnight. So I wanted to finalise some agreements before he goes back to the States tonight."

Theresa rolled her eyes. "Okay but I need an iced tea before I can start." They ordered a jug of iced lemon tea and some samosas and local snacks.

"Since our meeting in Prague, I was not sure if we would ever meet again," confessed Theresa. "In fact, I am not sure if we will ever get to see Toby again. I have not heard from him for a while. I texted to tell him that we are meeting today; he has not responded. I hope he is well. I remember very clearly what Monk Matt said that evening about time. Most of us know how much money we have left in our pockets or purses. We can even tell instantly the amount of money we have in our bank by using mobile apps. We live our lives knowing how much resources and money we have. However, do we really know how much time we have to live? No, we never know when our last day will be in this lifetime. It could be in thirty years or three days. Or it could be the in next three minutes. We never know. So we spend our entire lives trying to control it by knowing the unknown as much as we can. We know the weather, we know the flight departure and arrival to the precise moment, we know when an Uber car will arrive by looking at the app's GPS tracking, we know when our parcel will arrive through courier tracking codes. But we do not know how long our lives will last. So how we live our lives today is under the delusion that we have more time to do what we want to do. But do we have the time?"

Theresa sipped her iced tea, while Charles reflected on what she had just said, staring at the mint leaf perched on the edge of the tall glass. This was another reminder of the 'life is a prison' story which Antonio had told him about a few months ago.

His thoughts were interrupted by Theresa's next words. "A typical person works for eight hours, sleeps for eight hours, and spends eight hours on personal time."

Antonio interjected to lighten the mood. "That's not typical of Charles's schedule. He probably works for fifteen hours, sleeps for four, and spends the rest of the time travelling, in airports, doing other personal time for… what, four hours a day, yes?"

With a guilty smile, Charles sheepishly admitted, "That's about right."

Theresa continued, "And if a typical person lives up to seventy-five years of age, which is a person's average lifespan, then he would have spent twenty-five years sleeping, twenty-five years working, and twenty-five years on other activities. When you are fifty years old, Charles, you would have already lived two-thirds of your lifespan. You would only have twenty-five years to go. And based on Antonio's estimate of your daily time schedule, you would have been working for fifteen years and sleeping for five years, leaving about five years for your personal pursuits."

Charles had a shocked look on his face. "What? I am planning to retire and spend the money I had saved to enjoy the rest of my life. Five years is not enough time."

Theresa quipped sternly, "Enough time to do what? Most people have not figured out what matters most to them and what they really want to do when they retire. Doing nothing is not sustainable. The Life Inventory exercise will sort it out for you!"

Charles glanced nervously at his watch. "Will you guys be around tonight? I'd like to hear the full-blown version of this but it will take more time. I will buy dinner. My wife and I need to hear this. Actually, I need to know it more than Amy, but I would like Amy to be included so we can plan it together. Could you do this with me and my wife together? Maybe it could sort our lives out as well."

Antonio grinned, "We can do dinner. But only if that restaurant is at the top of Marina Bay Sands, overlooking the evening skyline of Singapore."

Charles laughed, "Deal! 7 p.m.? Meet me in the lobby on the ground floor."

Beep! Beep! Theresa's phone notified her of an incoming message. "Wait, wait! I just received a message from Toby. He writes, 'Hey Theresa! Sorry for not responding. Didn't have Internet access till today. Am in Bangkok in a monastery. Am a monk now. Original plan was to be a monk for thirty days, but it has been three months and I am still here. So much has happened to me since Prague. Tell you more if we meet again. Now learning to simplify my life and purify my inner mind. It's peaceful. Monk Matt was right, there are a lot of things we don't know about Karma. Hope Charles, Antonio, and you are all doing well. Will send my blessings to you all during meditations. Don't know when I will return to my old life. Maybe after the Rain Retreat, or maybe never. Live my life day by day now. Visit Wat Phra Dhammakaya if you can. Got to go for my afternoon chanting now. Send me text. Only check phone message once a week cos too much distraction. May you achieve peace and find happiness. Bye.'"

Beep! Beep! An image of Toby with a clean-shaven head, wearing yellow robes, looking like a younger version of Monk Matt came through. In the background were tall pine trees and some wooden huts. Theresa passed the phone around for them to see the picture of Toby.

Charles peered into the phone with a bewildered expression. "Wow! A monk! I think he's lost his mind already. Being a monk? He must have gone through a lot to make such a decision! Poor guy."

Theresa breathed deeply and exclaimed. "Good for Toby! He is the one who is on the right path. Whereas we are still here struggling with our delusion or trying to find happiness."

Antonio, still looking at the phone, said slowly, "He looks different. I mean besides the physical change, his eyes look calm and serene. I wish I could do that too… to give it all up and lead a monastic life, at least experience it for a short time. It will reboot my life totally."

Charles reflected on the note he had written after the meeting in Prague — 'Project Compassion: Check on Toby. He is in a difficult situation. Maybe I can help.' He felt a sense of guilt for his inaction.

Antonio broke the silence, "No Sex. Must be a big decision for him. Maybe we could visit Toby."

They all nodded in silence, but no one committed to a date or action.

8

TAKING CONTROL OF LIFE

In separation lies the world's great misery,
In compassion lies the world's true strength.

- Buddha -

WAT PHRA DHAMMAKAYA

Over the next few weeks, Charles was determined to make up for the shortfall of his first half business performance. He had a team of very capable General Managers and he planned to get them together for a working retreat to consolidate the execution plans. Charles was very good at orchestrating the execution of plans. He had been doing this for the past ten years as a business leader. His background as a Systems Engineer provided the systematic mindset. Designing and managing software development projects gave him the project management skills needed to manage complex teams and timelines. When he was promoted to lead sales and marketing, he developed the method to organise and drive sales through detailed execution plans.

This time, he had two items on his agenda. Firstly, he wanted to prove to his board that he was capable of turning his business around despite the economic downturn. By doing so, he would remain the top choice for any future promotions. He had been aiming for the promotion to Partner for some time. With this, he would be awarded with stocks that would get him his target financial personal net worth goal of $25 million.

Secondly, Charles wanted to have a chance to meet Monk Matt for advice to create his 'escape plan' from Greed, Delusion, and Anger. And if he could find Toby and convince him to come back to his normal life, that would be a bonus. In order to have all of these actions set in motion, Charles asked June, his personal assistant, to organise a Leadership Strategic Retreat weekend in Bangkok in January. He also asked Sandra, his Business Manager, to send out the standard Powerpoint template for all General Managers to present their execution plans. Charles knew that these managers were very good at creating twenty-page plans so he gave them parameters. He wanted only the essence in three pages and not lots of fluff. He decided to put all his experience together to create a methodology to help his team execute and achieve their plans this half.

Bangkok, January
Charles decided to treat Amy to a week of shopping in Bangkok. He invited her to be with him for a couple of days while he ran the weekend leadership retreat with his team. Amy was jubilant about the opportunity to get away from Singapore. She loved Bangkok and had some good friends who had relocated there. She set about contacting them to meet up for a weekend shopping spree and gossip session.

Meanwhile, Theresa had managed to locate Monk Matt at the Monastery. Monk would be able to meet Charles at the temple and spend time with him. Theresa also sent messages to Toby on his phone, but did not get any response from him.

Day 1. Charles and Amy rushed to get to the Singapore Changi International Airport. Amy managed to arrange for the kids to stay over with their friends for the week. She was excited to travel with her husband and enjoyed seeing him so happy. Charles tried to keep a relaxed mood, but inwardly, his mind was busy developing his presentation. He was excited to have an action-packed weekend as Charles loved being busy. It made him feel significant.

Day 2. The taxi arrived at the Wat Phra Dhammakaya and drove into the huge compound after a brief stop at the security gate. It was like driving into the Disneyland theme park — it was huge! When Charles looked around, it did not remind him of a typical Thai temple. There were no ornate structures with golden pointed roofs and statues of scary-looking creatures amidst celestial figurines donned in gold. The taxi had to slow down several times to allow groups of monks to cross the roads as they moved from building to building. Finally, the taxi stopped in front of a building that was shaped like a giant concrete globe, which reminded Charles of the geodesic sphere called Spaceship Earth at Walt Disney's Epcot in Florida. This was the Centennial Building, the world headquarters of the Dhammakaya Foundation, designed to be the World Center for Dhamma Studies and Peace.

As Charles alighted from the taxi, a tall lanky young monk approached him and asked. "Mr. Charles Watanabe?" Charles was pleasantly surprised with this reception, as if they were expecting him. The security guard had informed the international affairs office of a foreign visitor. Charles, still awed by the size of the concrete globe, replied, "Yes, that is me. I am here to meet Monk… err… Luang Phi… Matt."

The younger monk gestured Charles towards the entrance. "I am Luang Phi Timothy or Monk Tim. My role is to introduce our temple to international visitors and take them on a tour of its facilities."

Charles smiled, "Thank you! Do you have many visitors here?"

"Every week we have visitors," said Monk Tim. "They come from all over the world — USA, Japan, China, Singapore, Malaysia, and Europe. That's why I am assigned to this role as I speak English, Thai, Chinese, Japanese, French, and Spanish."

Charles was impressed. He followed Monk Tim into the building, through some hallways until they finally entered an open grass courtyard with a pond filled with lotus flowers. There were lots of trees providing shade and round stone tables with stools scattered around the park. Charles could see monks sitting at some of these tables. They seemed to be discussing matters related to the books in front of them.

Monk Tim explained, "These are novice monks. They attend classes on Buddhism, take exams on the Pāli language, and learn meditation daily." Monk Tim pointed to a nearby empty table under a large banyan tree. "You may wait here for Luang Phi Matt. He is finishing a class and will meet you in a few minutes. Meanwhile, you can enjoy the quiet environment or you may want to meditate while waiting."

Charles sat down at the table. Just looking around this serene environment was already very calming for him. He gazed around, observing the long vines hanging from the banyan tree over the pond. Leaves floated down to the pond, creating gentle ripples on the surface. His mind drifted to a time when he was a kid sitting by the lakeside fishing with his father. They used to fish for bass. His family had a small wooden cabin near a lake not far from his grandfather's house near Osaka. He loved fishing and his grandpa was a very kind man. After grandpa died, grandma passed away a year later. His father owned a small ramen shop at a food alley in the district of Shinsekai. Every day, Dad would wake up early, at 6 a.m., to prepare the noodles and he never came home before 1 a.m. Charles rarely had time to speak with his father as the latter was always working. Sigh! It seemed that his life in the corporate world was more complex and different from his dad's ramen shop, but a stark similarity is that their careers consumed so much of their time that they both did not have much time with their family.

Monk Matt broke Charles's reverie. "Hello, Charles."

Charles turned, smiled widely, and wanted to hug Monk but held back as he thought that it may not be the correct protocol to greet a monk. Monk Matt grabbed Charles's hand and held it warmly with both of his hands, and said, "How are you doing, Charles?"

"I am well mostly," replied Charles, "but very stressed. I need some advice. That's why I am here to meet you… err… I mean to meet Monk Matt again." Charles suddenly remembered that he should not to use 'I' or 'you' when referring to Monk.

Monk Matt, still holding Charles's hands, shook it lightly while looking gently into his eyes. He said warmly, "Monk knows everything will be all right. Let's talk more later. First Monk would like to show you around the temple grounds." Just then, an electric buggy pulled up along the path as they turned. "Let's take a ride. We will go around the temple and then end up at the ordination headquarters where we can have some coffee or tea."

Charles was impressed with the immense size of the temple grounds. They visited the novice monk training centre, the living quarters, the laundry area, and the dinner hall. The place was very organised and sparkling clean. Charles visited the main Meal Hall, where two thousand monks can be fed under one roof. Then he saw the Meditation Hall that could fit five hundred thousand people, and the Temple 'Stadium' that could accommodate one million people meditating at the same time. In the centre of the stadium was a massive golden dome with a saucer-shaped wing span of about 400 metres in diameter called the Cetiya. A Cetiya refers to 'reminders' or 'memorials', which are objects or places used by Theravada Buddhists to remember Gautama Buddha. It is an amazing sight when viewed from afar. At night, when the light shines on the one million golden Buddha statues on the dome, it generates a golden glow that creates a light beam up to the sky. Monk Matt explained the history of the temple and about the Grand Master Luang Pu — which means the venerable grandfather — who rediscovered Buddha's lost ancient method of meditation called Dhammakaya Meditation. Hence this place was named the Dhammakaya temple, or the Dhammakaya Meditation Center.

Said Monk Matt, "Today, meditation is taught here as a means to achieve inner peace for individuals, monks, or laypeople, who in turn will share loving kindness with the community we live in, hence achieving more peace around us. This practice of Buddhism differs from Japan, China, or Taiwan. Here it focuses on meditation as the focal point towards the improvement of society. It is called Theravada Buddhism which is based on the original records of the Buddha scripture, or Sutra. Theravada is practised mainly in South East Asia, including Thailand, Bangladesh, and Sri Lanka. In Mahayana Buddhism, which is practised in China, Taiwan, and Hong Kong, it focuses on spreading the Dhamma, which are teachings of Buddha as the main propagation of the religion. Meditation is practised as a secondary support to Dhamma sharing."

"What are they chanting over there?" Charles asked, referring to the people holding lotus flowers, walking along the tracks that circumambulate the Cetiya.

Monk answered, "They are chanting the first sermon of Lord Buddha, called the Dhammacakkappavattana Sutra. This is the most significant sermon of all Buddha's sermons as it was the first teaching of Buddha after he achieved enlightenment. It's from this sermon that Buddha taught the four noble truths and the path to escape the cycle of suffering so that one would attain Nirvana."

Charles asked, "Suffering refers to pain, loss, failure, unhappiness, and negative results?"

Monk nodded, "Yes, these are suffering, and more. Being born begins the cycle of suffering for a person. Ageing is suffering. Sickness is suffering. Dying is suffering. Any bodily sensation will eventually lead to suffering. The six senses cause one to like or dislike, feel if something is pleasurable or unpleasurable, experience victory or defeat. All this leads to suffering. The sensations of taste, smell, and even good thoughts are impermanent and will turn into the opposite sensations. All these are sufferings. Buddha says nothing is permanent, every moment things change, time does not stop. Hence if we are attached to any thing, any feelings or expectations, they will not remain in this state. When we try to control and keep things the same, we are deluding ourselves. For example, we miss our loved ones when they pass away. That's holding on to feelings of happiness when they were alive. By reminding us of those happy days, we feel sad, remorse, or regret that we could not hold on to it forever. That is suffering. Another example is the joy of owning a brand new car. The feeling of pride arises from the smell of new leather and the admiration of the beautiful perfect gloss of the body work. Imagine what happens when you return to the carpark to find an ugly scratch at the side panel of your brand new pride. It invokes anger, rage, and frustration. That is suffering."

Charles commented, "If every day is perfect, then there would be no suffering and life would be heaven on earth, right?"

Monk smiled, "You know that such a perfect state cannot exist on earth because most humans are self-preserving by nature, which leads to self-centredness. Greed is developed by the demands for comfort, excessive needs, and societal pressure. The first sermon also teaches The Eightfold Path to end suffering."

Charles was curious. "What is that?"

Monk explained, "The Eightfold Path are principles that guide us to the cessation of suffering. The principles to have are:

1. Right View;
2. Right Thought;
3. Right Speech;
4. Right Action;
5. Right Effort;
6. Right Livelihood;
7. Right Mindfulness; and
8. Right Concentration."

"This seems like a very practical philosophy to being successful in anything we do," said Charles. "Is there a book or any literature I could read more about the Eightfold Path and the Four Noble Truths?"

Monk nodded, "Yes, let Monk take you to the library later. There are some books that you could borrow."

Charles could immediately relate to some of these principles as they were so simple and self-explanatory. He liked these principles because they were the exact attitudes he expected his team to practise and take the steps to exceed their business results. Charles's mind was working very fast and mentally, he began to develop a framework to create a business methodology of execution for success. Such brilliant moments of insights occurred to Charles many times throughout his life. This was one such brainwave moment where ideas get formulated into structures and frameworks by combining concepts and ideas into solutions. This was the genesis of a methodology that he would later call 'The Results Pathway'. It consisted of taking The Four Right Steps along a pathway to success:

Step 1.
See Right. Look at situation with a 360-degree perspective. Give and seek feedback from others.

Step 2.
Think Right. Engage in positive self-thought instead of engaging in negative self-thought. Refrain from making assumptions but verify thoughts with facts that are supported by comprehensive perspectives from See Right.

Step 3.
Say Right. Say things that are useful, helpful, and constructive instead of things which disparage others, and are untruthful and untimely.

Step 4.

Act Right. Do the right thing. Taking action based on good intentions. Act in the rightful manner to support the steps of See Right, Think Right, and Say Right.

When people Think and Act above the Pathway, they commit to what they can do, why it must happen, by when, and focus on solutions. They explore the reasons, feel empowered, and take the Four Right Steps leading them up the Pathway to Success.

On the contrary, not taking the right steps would result in a path to failure. The opposite of these Four Right Steps was engaging in Blame Actions which was accusing others, pointing fingers, covering up, confusion, ignorance, and denial. When people Think and Act below the Pathway, they state what cannot be done, why it did not happen, and focus on the problem. They make excuses, felt victimised, and get caught in the blame game cycle, spiralling down the Pathway to Failure.

Monk Matt's phone buzzed. He took the call and spoke to someone in Thai.

While Monk was speaking on the phone, Charles took the chance to do a quick sketch of his Results Pathway framework, which he wanted to use for his weekend Leadership Strategic Retreat.

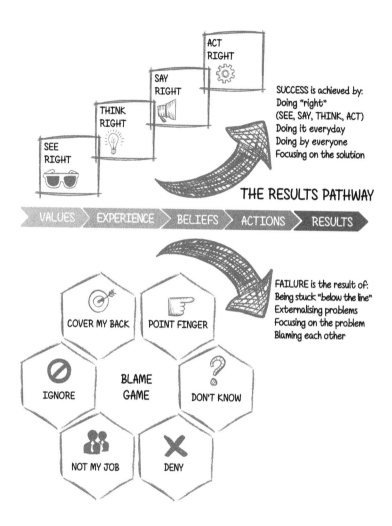

IDOP VILLAGE

"Let's visit the IDOP Village," suggested Monk. "IDOP
stands for International Dhammadayada Ordination
Program. It is the training ground for all foreign nationals
who choose to be ordained as monks."

The buggy turned away from one of the north-east corners of the temple stadium square and stopped near a forested area. The entrance had a sliding wooden gate. Monk Matt reminisced about the time, about ten years ago, when he came to the temple to join the thirty-day ordination programme. Most of the temple grounds were unpaved and the training camp sites were next to the river. There were very few trees because this land, which was donated by a wealthy businesswoman, was arid and the soil were very acidic. Very few plants could survive in those conditions. Through years of experimentation and input from monks who were graduates in agricultural studies, they learnt to grow plants that could withstand such natural soil conditions. Additionally, they also learnt how to nourish the soil through composting techniques and proper irrigation methods.

"This is our last tour stop," said Monk Matt. "This is the IDOP Village, where I spend a lot of time giving Dhamma talks to newly ordained monks."

They got off the buggy and walked inside the compound. It had walking paths between the trees and manicured grass areas. There were single-storey buildings at the far end, and four rows of small wooden huts along the fringe of the forested compound. A large lake was on one side and a light-wooded area on the other. There were monks walking in small groups of two or three. At the far end of the paths was a group of young monks walking in two neat lines away from them. Monk Matt took a left path towards a sheltered meditation pavilion with no walls. At one end of the hall was a raised stage platform with a man-sized statue of Buddha in meditation posture.

"This is one of the meditation halls where we conduct afternoon sessions," explained Monk. "All the residents in this village are going through intensive basic training to be a monk. Some are here for thirty days, some are here for three months or longer. It depends on their goals. Our Abbott wanted to provide this facility for men who are interested to experience the life of a monk at least once in their lifetime. We do not have female monks here. We built this facility for international, non-Thai nationals, to receive intensive training to prepare them for ordination as well as to be trained to live the life of a Dhammakaya monk."

Suddenly Charles remembered Toby, so he asked, "So is Toby here as well?"

Monk smiled, "Let's take a seat inside this hall and have some refreshments."

They sat at one end of the hall where there were some chairs next to a small long table. A man in a white uniform came with tea, coffee, and bottled water. Charles was relieved to have his boost of caffeine. Then he noticed a few young monks walking by the hall. They were walking in silence maintaining a calm rhythm in their pace. They stopped in front of the hall, spoke a little, then one of them turned towards the hall. He removed his sandals, arranged it neatly at the edge of the steps in a slow deliberate motion then started to approach them. Charles just looked at him, assuming that he was looking for Monk Matt.

Instead of facing Monk, this young monk walked towards Charles and said. "Hello Charles, long time no see." Charles was shocked. But there was something familiar about the voice. He looked at the monk and began to recognise the familiar smile and face of Toby. Yet something looked different. Of course! With no hair, the face looked so plain and clean. Then he realised that Toby had no eyebrows as well. Now his senses confirmed that this was the Toby who looked thinner and more serene than the Toby in Prague.

"Don't you recognise me, Charles?" the young monk asked.

"Toby!" cried Charles. "Oh my gosh! It's really you, Toby! No, I almost didn't recognise you without the curly hair, your eyebrows, and… and… you've lost so much weight!"

Charles stood up and reached his hands outwards to grab Toby for a hug. Toby hugged him back and they both enjoyed the presence of each other like old friends. "So Monk Matt," said Charles, "you knew about this all along and you planned this surprise?"

Monk smiled, "After receiving a text from Theresa that Toby had become a monk in Thailand, Luang Phi was not sure where Toby was at first. He could be with any of the fifty thousand temples in Thailand. While there are other temples that conduct monk ordination, IDOP provides the best English ordination programme for non-Thai nationals, so Luang Phi started to search for Toby in this temple. There are three thousand resident monks here, but the temple keeps a registry. It was just a matter of checking. It was only 10 minutes ago when Luang Phi received a phone call from the working committee confirming that Toby was here."

Toby was beaming. "I cannot express how happy I am to see you all again. I have so much to tell you." Toby, upon seeing Charles, had dropped his guard and forgotten that a monk does not refer to himself as 'I' or 'me'. This often happens to newly-ordained monks because they find it odd replacing 'I' with 'Luang Phi' or 'Monk' when referring to themselves, especially when speaking with people they have been very familiar with in the past.

Charles urged Toby, "Please tell us what happened to you since we left Prague."

"Toby stayed with me for a month in Prague helping Luang Phi with the meditation programme," said Monk Matt. "He was very helpful as his technical and computer skills was just what we needed at the Prague meditation workshops. When we separated in Prague, Toby told Luang Phi that his plan was to return to Malaysia and get back to his dance studio. Toby did not give any indication of his interest to be a monk."

ESCAPING DEATH

They all sat down and Toby started telling the story of his rocky journey after his return to Malaysia.

After the chance meeting in Prague where Toby bumped into Antonio and later joined Monk Matt for lunch under that tree, Toby stayed in Prague for another month. Since his luggage was lost and he had no money because he was pickpocketed, he offered to help Monk Matt with his workshops. The organiser offered to put Toby up in a small room at one of the volunteer's house. He would wake up at 4 a.m. every morning to prepare for the day's schedule for Monk. Toby was handy with technology and he was the perfect person to fiddle with the setting up of the computers, audio-visual and projector systems, as well as any technical stuff. He suddenly became a very valuable resource throughout the event and that made Toby feel very good. During the one month travelling and helping Monk Matt, he learnt to meditate. Through meditation, Toby learnt to be calm, breathing techniques, and how to keep his mind still. Miraculously, after two weeks, the airport returned his luggage and the insurance company compensated him €100 per day for his delayed luggage. That came up to a total of €1,400 which was more than the price of his flight ticket. The local police also managed to recover his wallet. A staff at the Hemingway Bar found his wallet next to a rubbish bin in the back alley. Of course the money and credit cards were missing, but Toby managed to retrieve his identity card and the note containing his friend's contact, whom he was supposed to meet in Prague for a job.

This trip to Prague had turned in an unexpected direction. Instead of getting a job here, he became the assistant to a Monk. His meditation improved and he was able to listen to the Dhamma talks by Monk about Karma and other principles of living, being content, and finding happiness.

Toby told Charles, "Before Prague, I could not control my life. Everything I did since leaving high school was dictated by other people around me. I did not go to college because I spent so much time helping my dad in his dance studio. It's not his fault though. I liked dancing so much that my goal as a teenager was to be the best dancer in the world. Also, being a good dancer gets you chicks! I could get physically close to girls while teaching them dancing. Being a national junior dance champion gave me a lot of attention from pretty girls. My grades at high school were not good enough to get into the local university. Since Dad could not afford to send me to a college in the US, I worked as a dance instructor at his studio to save for my own college fund. I became a regional dance champion and spent a lot of time competing in overseas events in Asia. There were many wealthy mature ladies who engaged me to be their dance partner at competitions. The generous tips and expensive hotels became my lifestyle. I drank and smoked every night. The only thing I did not do was drugs. We competed in Moscow, Paris, Shanghai, and at all the major dance events. I started drinking a lot because of the stress at work. After I came out of rehab, I went to Prague and met you guys."

Toby sighed deeply, as if he had just relived the most painful part of his life.

Monk commented, "You were very sober when you spent that four weeks with Luang Phi in Prague."

Charles looked at Toby, "After our meeting in Prague, I told myself to contact you and offer some help. But, stupid me, I got totally consumed by my work and forgot about the whole thing. I felt so guilty. In fact, I never made it to Monk Matt's talk that evening."

He gave Monk Matt an apologetic look. "I was at my company's awards dinner and could not peel away from that event. We won several awards and people just wanted to celebrate and take photos. After several bottles of champagne and wine, I lost track of time. I flew off the next day. But that's another story that I can tell you about later. To keep it short, I never executed those personal commitments I made after listening to Monk Matt's advice at the park. I wrote them down but that's all I did. No, wait, I did call my mum and have a wonderful lunch with her. And Amy and I had a wonderful talk about my plan to retire from corporate life.

"Then the busy schedule sucked me back into my normal cycle of existence, until three weeks ago when I had the visit from Antonio and Theresa in Singapore. They woke me up from this 'auto-pilot' mode. I decided to take control of things and not let things take control of me again. And my first act of taking control of my life was to plan a trip to meet Monk Matt this week. That is the short version."

"Hey, I appreciate your thoughts of helping me," said Toby. "I didn't know that you would even think of me as worthy of your time. But thanks! As it turns out, my four weeks with Monk Matt set me up for a reset of my life. In computer geek jargon, it was a 'hard reset.'"

Charles and Monk Matt nodded in unison. "Tell us what led you to decide to be a monk," said Charles.

Toby took a deep breath, a sip of water, then shifted his sitting position to make himself comfortable. He closed his eyes, took another two breaths deeply and slowly, reopened his eyes gently, and kept a slight smile before he continued.

"With €1,400 in my pocket from the insurance claim, I bought a one-way ticket home. Everyone's lives at home had gone on as if I was never there. Of course, my dad was very pleased to see me. Immediately, he was ready to refer new dance customers to restart my career. I had dinner with my wife and kids, hoping for a reconciliation. The dinner was strange and quiet. My wife was seeing another man named Tommy. During the kids' conversations, I overheard them saying 'Uncle Tommy this' and 'Uncle Tommy that'. It seemed that he had integrated into the family well. I was jealous and angry at my wife for her infidelity and we ended up having a big shouting match. I stormed out of the house and went back to Dad's house. My apartment was under joint ownership with my wife but since she and the kids were staying there, I was essentially homeless!

"I tried to get back into a routine and decided to take control of my career. I sold my share of the studio to my wife and received $50,000 in cash in settlement. She did not want to fight me anymore, so she paid me the price that I asked for and never negotiated a cent less. I respect her for that. Then I indulged in competitive dancing. I trained hard for World Dance Championship in Hong Kong. At first, I was ostracised by the professional dancers who used to be my compatriots and friends. I could understand why as it was bad business for them to be associated with a 'psycho' who was an ex-mental hospital patient. I changed from being an alcoholic to being a workaholic. Slowly I began to garner respect from the younger and newer generation of dancers who were trained in Korean dance schools. I learnt new moves and became really good. I got my mojo back and began to win some local competitions. Then I started to win some regional competitions too. I became so focused and competitive that my wife's affair didn't bother me. I was motivated and had the fire in me. Financially it was tough as I had to survive on the payout for the studio to fund my competitions and travels. The funds started to dry up quickly. I was not earning much because I taught only beginner's dance classes. I did not want to be distracted by advanced students who needed a lot of time and attention. My father gave me some ad-hoc dance projects to sustain my own living. It was really stressful when I was preparing for the world competition. Trained eight hours a day. Taught five hours a day. For three months, I trained non-stop and that schedule became my life.

"During the competition I danced the best moves I ever did and made no mistakes, yet, I lost. I came in second runner-up. For most people, that's a great come back after not being competitive for a few years. But for me, I was not satisfied. I became depressed and started drinking again. I felt like a failure. I went back to coaching other dancers, to help them train to participate in competitions. I hated that job. My anger and jealousy for my wife and her lover returned, and it overwhelmed me. I engaged a private detective to check on her and wanted to file for divorce and get custody of my kids and half of my apartment. I was angry all the time.

"During this period, my most sympathetic and compassionate friends were the owners of the bars that I frequented. They bought me free drinks and showered me with lots of young hostesses every night. I brought them back to my dad's dance studio and had wild parties after the bars closed. One day, Dad called me to his office and gave me a long lecture. Even though he had been hard on me, he had always supported me. But this time, he expressed grave disappointment at my behaviour. He told me that if I didn't sober up and get back to my normal life, he did not want me in his studio or his house anymore. He had to clean up the studio every morning after my parties; and having to clean the toilet of puke and condoms was not what a 72-year-old man wanted to do.

"That afternoon, I called the bar owners to pour out my sorrows. We drank the whole day. By nightfall, we were so drunk that we laughed at everything that moved. I felt very happy. That's the last thing I remember.

"The next day, my 8 a.m. student, Jessy, found me lying on my dad's studio sofa. Jessy was one of the smartest and prettiest students in my class. I could tell that she really liked me, but I was not ready to get into a serious relationship then. Even though I was separated from my wife, we were technically still married. I had given Jessy the studio door access combination code because she would come in early to get the studio ready then do her warm-up practices. Some days, she would close the studio for me after her evening class. That morning, Jessy could not wake me up and noticed me foaming at the mouth. She was training to be a nurse, so she had an idea what had happened. After checking my pulse and my eyes, she called the emergency hotline.

"What actually happened, as I realised later, was that I had had alcohol poisoning, and my organs were shutting down one by one. In fact, according to the medical report, at the hospital, my heart stopped for 3 minutes before they were able to revive me. They had to clean out the alcohol from my blood. The next few hours were the most torturous of my life. Nurses pumped my stomach by flushing liquid through my mouth and nose. That process was repeated over and over again in order to get the alcohol out of my system. Jessy stayed at my bedside throughout. Each time

I woke up I saw her angelic face, before I dozed off again.
I was never conscious for more than a few minutes. They
could not maintain my consciousness completely and my
body started to shut down again. Then I went into a coma.
Everyone thought I was going to die.

"At one point, I remember hearing a sweet voice
singing and a gentle breeze blowing over my face. I knew
I was in heaven. A soft hand had taken hold of mine and
was leading me. I held on and wanted to follow this angel
to wherever she wanted to take me. That's when I woke
up from my coma. That was three weeks after I passed
out. Jessy was singing the song to me. It was the song that
we competed to in one of the local dance competitions.
She was holding my hand as if we were doing that waltz
again. We came in second place at that competition. It was
her first win. She was jubilant, while I was upset at her
imperfect steps.

"After I woke up from my coma, Jessy told me the
whole chronology of events. I was so ashamed of myself
that I broke down and cried. Over the next few days, while
recuperating, all I heard were reprimands from my dad,
my aunt, and my wife. Even my drinking buddies came.
They were guilty and remorseful. My three kids came to
visit me but were standing at the corner of the room, busy
texting on their phones. Some dance students came with
flowers and good wishes.

"While lying in the hospital, I recalled Monk Matt's
teaching on meditation. Every night before I slept, I

meditated for 30–45 minutes. Then I meditated every time I was alone. It started to help me recover. I would see a bright light whenever I meditated and felt light and bright."

THE FUNERAL

Toby continued with his story. "One evening, I was so depressed and fed up by all the visitors, I decided to ask for permission to go to the rooftop garden of the hospital to breathe some fresh air. I found a quiet spot there and sat down to meditate. That evening, the sky was clear after a good rain. The sun was golden orange. A few minutes into meditation, I became very relaxed. Then I found myself at a funeral parlour. I saw my friends and relatives engaged in animated conversation. Then I realised that the person in the coffin was me! They were all talking about me. While I could not hear what they were saying, I could feel that they were disappointed with me. I did not sense any compassion or sympathy. Even my father seemed angry with me for being dead. My children were very sad. They looked guilty and regretful as they stood over the coffin. I was just watching from above and was not trying to get involved or change their minds. I was very calm and unmoved by their emotions. For once in my life, I was unaffected by all their opinions, criticism, or feelings of anger, disappointments, shame, or guilt. I felt dispassionate and was just floating in the air around that scene."

"Antonio gave me a word to describe that," said Charles. "It's called equanimous. Equanimity is a state of calmness and composure, especially in difficult situations."

Monk Matt added, "Equanimity is one of the four paths to condition the mind to attain happiness. Laypeople refer to it as the four ideal attitudes to achieve happiness. The other paths or attitudes are Love, Compassion, and Sympathetic Joy. What Toby experienced was, indeed, a state of equanimity."

Toby nodded in acknowledgement of what Monk Matt had said. "I didn't know how to interpret that vision. It felt like a dream, but I was fully aware of the environment around me, and I was not asleep. When the nurse came to take me back downstairs, she interrupted my meditation session. When I was back in my room, I remembered what Monk Matt said about the highway to Nirvana. Luang Phi Matt, could you tell Charles that highway story again?"

"Of course," replied Monk. "While both laypeople and monks are humans who live on earth, they have very different purposes in their lives. Laypeople's lives are filled with work commitments, personal desires, studies, and the pursuit of success. They own cars, houses, materials things, and are stressed by relationships, sadness, love, and hatred. Their purpose in life is to be happy and that's the road they take to achieve happiness. Monks' purposes are also to achieve ultimate happiness, but their roads are different.

"Monks search for happiness with the purpose of achieving Nirvana. They live a simple life with few possessions. They eat one or two meals a day and do not have to work for a livelihood. Their meals are donated. Their robes are donated. Their huts, or Kuti, are only 2.7 metres by 1.6 metres in size. Monks start their day at 4.30 a.m. and sleep by 10 p.m. They meditate and chant sutras three to four times a day. Monks observe 227 precepts to ensure that their conduct is maintained at the utmost of wholesomeness. Because of this, their paths towards ultimate happiness, or Nirvana, is faster than laypeople's. They are on the fast lane of the super highway. No traffic jams and no traffic lights."

Toby chipped in, "That's the highway I wanted to take to get out of my unhappiness. That's why I decided to be ordained as a monk."

"What happened to Jessy," asked Charles, "your kids, your father, and the studio business? Who's responsible for them now?"

"At that moment, with my near-death experience, I was willing to give up everything," said Toby. "Nobody was happy with me when I was alive, and nobody seemed to be happy with me in the vision of my own funeral during meditation. So I figured it didn't matter. One evening, Jessy came to visit me after her nursing classes. She was the only one who genuinely showed concern for me. I did not want to enter into a relationship with her and drag her into my messy life. So I asked her how she would feel if I decided to go away to a faraway place, far from everyone and not come back for a long time. She cried, thinking that

I was planning to commit suicide. She said she wanted to take care for me, and she did not care what other people thought of me."

Toby wiped a tear from his eye. "I told her that I was not going to die but had decided to be ordained as a monk in Thailand. She cried even more, as she felt that being a monk is as bad as losing me forever. I explained to her that I wanted to find myself from inside. I had been looking outside for meaning and purpose, and all I found were unrealistic expectations from others that I could not fulfil. The more I tried, the worse mess I got myself into. I told Jessy that I needed to clean myself from inside out and that I was a broken man. I could not even take care of myself, so would not be good for her. Jessy cried louder but promised to wait for me. I gave her all my trophies and told her to complete her nursing degree and help more people. If we are meant to be together, it would happen. If I didn't return from the monastery, then maybe we would meet again in our next life and be together then. She saved me from death, so it must be my good karma."

Toby paused to control his emotions. "I referred all my dance clients to my wife. I asked her for forgiveness. And I had a man-to-man talk with Tommy and wished them well. I signed the divorce papers to free her from our marriage obligations. I signed my share of the apartment to my kids. So that's how it happened."

Charles heaved a sigh of relief.

Monk Matt said, "There are no coincidences, and nothing happens by accident in our lifetime. How our life turns out is the result of past habits, retribution and rewards from actions we had taken. When we go through life with the mindset of self-centredness, being jealous or envious of others' success, plotting crafty ways to beat the 'system', or harbouring past hatred and anger, then our lives will be filled with difficulties ahead. So Toby's decision to be a monk to 'clean himself from inside out' would help to build good karma."

Monk Matt noticed that Toby was taking shallow breaths in a slow rhythmic manner. He knew that Toby was entering a conscious meditative state while paying attention to the conversation. Monk thought to himself: *This is good. Toby is able to centre his mind to a state of stillness so that the mind does not wander. When the mind is still, thoughts are reduced, and the mind comes into the centre of the body to rest. This is when wisdom can be attained as deeper insights.*

Monk Matt continued, "Many people think that karma is fate, or something closely tied to it. You often hear them say, 'She must have some bad or good karma.' They talk about karma like it is some sort of invisible currency. If you do the right thing, good things will come back to you as a reward. If you do the wrong thing, bad things will come back to you as a punishment. Karma is actually not fate. Karma refers to intentional thoughts, words, and actions, and the energy created by these thoughts, words, and actions. Our thoughts and intentions are the building blocks to how the future road ahead of us will be constructed. Just by thinking of something begins an intention. Good intentions will lead to good actions that invoke good karmic effect. Bad intentions that lead to bad actions will invoke bad karmic effects.

"It is the effect, or the result of the actions, that are the consequences we suffer or enjoy. There are people who work hard all their lives, yet they encounter bad luck, or constantly fall prey to deceitful schemes, or are victimised by politics at work. This is the result of the karma from their past lives. On the other hand, when we rejoice in the success of others, sympathise with the misfortune of others, and make good wishes for self and others, perform wholesome deeds, develop a compassionate mind, and commit to charity to help others in need, we will eventually experience good outcomes as these are good karmic actions. Being 'lucky' is the result of our previous volitions or intentional actions. That's sometimes also referred to as the Natural Law of Attraction. Good energy attracts good outcome. Bad energy attracts negative outcomes."

Toby's eyes were half-closed as if he was in a state of trance. Slowly his eyes opened and he spoke. "My life is simple here. My possessions are only four items: robe, bowl, small wooden hut, and medicine. Nobody judges me for what I do or do not do. I've learnt about how to do wholesome deeds to accumulate merits. These karma, which are intentional actions, is the law that guides my behaviour. I had never believed in this karma stuff before. I used to think that I could take control of my life by acting and behaving in ways that give me satisfaction and fulfilment. But I was doing it all wrong.

"I spent six months in rehab for my alcoholism. Then I went away to Prague for a month. When I returned home, I noticed that everyone's life had gone on as usual. My 'disappearance' did not impact them at all. In fact, I believe that without me, it was easier for my dad, my ex-wife, and my children. They were better off without me. I was the one who was miserable when I was with them and caused their miseries as well. Being a monk helped them and myself. Perfecto!"

Charles finally understood the impact of Toby's decision to be a monk, for himself as well as for the people around him. It was a responsible decision, which was the opposite of Charles's perception of ordination as an act of escapism from reality and being irresponsible.

Toby continued, "The past three months as a monk has helped me gain three key realisations. Firstly, I do not need to live up to anyone's expectations. My own expectation is to be a good righteous monk and live by the 227 precepts every day. Secondly, meditation helps my mind to be pure and clear. Without desires and attachments, my mind is freed from the defilements of pleasure, sadness, guilt, disappointment, and other sense-desires that affect my happiness. And thirdly, by learning about the Law of Karma, I have realised that I had done lots of bad karma stuff, like drinking excessively, sexual promiscuity, use of bad language, and having ill-will thoughts of others. Hence, I want to build up good merits through the acts of good wholesome deeds. While good actions do not negate the bad actions that I have committed, at least I can accumulate more good merits to reduce the impact of my previous bad karma acts."

Charles's original objective was to find Toby and convince him that he needed to go home. But now, he could see that Toby was a lot more relaxed and in control of his own happiness. His state of calmness and serenity was a total transformation. Toby had rescued himself. Charles realised that his own life purpose needed a rescue plan.

Charles was curious about something Toby said. "Why doesn't good karma negate bad karma? I assumed that when we do more good deeds, it would wipe out the effects of bad karma, no?"

Toby explained, "No. It is not a zero-sum game. It's not an equation where Good Karma minus Bad Karma equals Net Karma."

Charles was not convinced. "So, whatever good deeds we do now do not negate the bad deeds that we did before? That's pretty harsh. Why would a habitual bad person be motivated to turn around to do good?"

Monk Matt elaborated, "Imagine an unwholesome deed like a spoon of salt. Committing an unwholesome act is like adding salt to a bucket of water. Our Karma Bucket stores all the good and bad fruits of our karmic actions. The bucket of water will taste salty as we add more salt. When we do good wholesome deeds, we add more pure water into this bucket. A person's Karma Bucket can taste very salty if he has done lots of unwholesome deeds, or less salty if he has done more wholesome deeds. If a bad person decides only to do pure wholesome deeds for the rest of his life, he will only be diluting his Karma Bucket with more pure water, and over time, the water in the bucket would taste less salty. The salt content never disappears; it just gets diluted by the amount of pure water."

"We don't have a lot of time left in this lifetime," said Toby. "I want to add more pure water into my Karma Bucket so that all the past saltiness will get diluted. And by being a monk, I am taking the express lane to do more wholesome deeds."

Turning to Toby, Charles made a feeble attempt to get Toby back to normal life, "Toby, when you are done being a monk and are ready to come back home, let me know, I would like to start on a project with you." Charles did not have any idea what the project would be, but he just said it out of an unknown gut feeling.

CRABS IN A BASKET

Toby shook his head. "I am not going back to my old life for a while because it is too complicated. Being a monk is so peaceful. My life is simple and there is so much to learn. Every day, we have three sessions to learn the teachings of Buddha from more experienced monks who want to impart their knowledge. I practise meditation at least four times a day as part of a group. I can do walking meditation whenever I feel sleepy in the afternoons. I have daily access to mentor monks who are always willing to coach me. Being a monk is very good cleansing for me. I am learning to empty my cup. My cup was filled with so much past experiences and events that triggers negatives thoughts inside me. Hatred, anger, sadness, guilt, shame and disappointment. I was leading a life that was delusional. My life used to be like crabs crawling in a basket."

Charles looked puzzled. Monk Matt gave a quizzical look.

"Have you ever been to a market where they sell seafood?" asked Toby.

Charles replied, "Yes, I grew up in a small fishing village back in Japan. But that was a long time ago."

"In the market where they sell live seafood, crabs are kept inside bamboo baskets," said Toby. "This allows the crabs to stay alive longer as the crabs at the bottom can breathe from the sides. If you observe them for a while, you will notice that when one crab tries to climb up the wall of the basket, another crab will use the first crab as leverage to climb higher. Then a third will do the same until the weight of all the climbing crabs will cause all of them to fall back into the basket. After a while, another will try again, and the same behaviour will be repeated. As such, no crabs will be successful in escaping from the basket."

Charles nodded.

Toby said, "Life for me was like that those crabs in the basket. Each time I tried something new, the burden of other expectations from people around me would weigh on my shoulders. Why couldn't people just leave me alone to do what I wanted to do? But their opinions, suggestions, demands, and advice would always pull me back into the 'basket'. Of course, I could have chosen not to listen to them, but I guess that's my weakness. The more people cared for me, the more I sought their approval. So I just complied.

"Anyway, back to the crab story. Soon all the crabs will be tired from the climbing and falling. Occasionally, there might be one crab who, despite the tiredness, will make one more attempt to climb when the other crabs are exhausted. It will then break free because there are no crabs clinging on to it. That crab is me. Being ordained as a monk is me breaking free from my old crab basket."

Charles loved Toby's analogy of the crabs in the basket. He planned to incorporate it into his opening speech for his Leadership Strategic Retreat that weekend.

Monk Matt thought that the story described the lives of many people who lived in delusion. Toby realised that being a monk only gave him the temporary relief of having escaped from the basket. There was a bigger basket which he needed to escape from. In fact, even when that lone crab escaped from the basket, the mighty hand of the shopkeeper could just pick it up and toss it into another basket. That is why human life is a cycle of countless rebirths. A person needed to understand this and take action to get out of this cycle of rebirth, called Samsara in Pāli. That is the enlightenment that Buddha has been teaching.

Monk Matt said, "Toby has discovered that he was living in a world of deception, where the attractions and distractions of the material world lead him away from happiness. Now Toby is taking action to change himself. That is wisdom. Through daily meditation, he will find deeper inner power, insight, and better clarity."

Charles sighed. "Toby, I am so happy to hear that you have found the way to escape from the vicious cycle of our daily material world. I am sure Antonio and Theresa will be very happy to learn about your decision. For me, I am stuck in my own 'hamster wheel' and I find it very hard to get out. I am envious of your brave decision to break free and be a monk. I wish I could give it all up and just lead a simple life like what you described."

Charles sighed again, this time deeper than before. "My responsibilities are immense and so many people's lives depend on me. My responsibility to my company, my commitment to my boss, and the hundred and twenty very loyal employees who have helped me build the company. I feel accountable to ensure that their careers are secure, especially this second half of the year when we are not hitting our targets. Many may lose their jobs if we don't recover our sales and market share. I have worked so hard to accumulate stock options, and if I leave today, I will forgo a huge sum of money. I wanted to save that money for my retirement.

"For my family, I want to see my kids through college, and that will take another seven years. After that, Amy, my wife, and I can probably downgrade our lifestyle, but that would require a significant conscious effort. I want to do it, but I need years to plan the exit. In fact, I told myself that I would retire from my job in three years' time. I wish there is a fast lane for this process for me."

A volunteer in a white uniform came to remind them that lunchtime for the monks would begin in 15 minutes, at 11.30 a.m. The buggy was ready to take them to the main Meal Hall. Toby would join the IDOP monks for their own lunch separately at the IDOP dining hall. Monk Matt and Toby both uttered to each other, "Sadhu!", a term commonly used to acknowledge an act of virtue. There were no emotional or excessive farewell gestures between the friends. Charles clasped his palms together in a praying hands gesture and bid Toby a final farewell. "Hey man, I mean Luang Phi Toby, take care and may you attain Nirvana soon." Toby replied with a quick and heartfelt blessing for Charles, and they parted.

9

CHARLES'S ESCAPE PLAN

Success is a lousy teacher.
It seduces smart people into thinking they can't lose.
- Bill Gates -

THREE KEYS QUESTIONS

Charles had some specific questions for Monk Matt. After lunch, Charles was with Monk in one of the quiet corners of The Central Library, on the floor of the Centennial globe-shaped building. From the window, there was a clear view of the Cetiya, serving as a reminder of Buddha.

This magnificent structure gave Charles a sense of awe. He wondered about the significance of that specific shape.

Charles thought: *This organisation has thought of every detail to promote meditation. They have monthly organised ordination programmes catering for Thai nationals, and annual programmes for international ordinands in Chinese, Japanese, and English. With over eighty international meditation centres around the world, the goal of the Abbot is to help individuals achieve inner peace through the unique technique of Dhammakaya meditation, ultimately promoting world peace. I'm sure there is a reason for the Cetiya.*

Monk Matt came to sit beside Charles. He maintained a slight smile all the time, a practice the Master Abbot taught all monks. The Master Abbot had said, "When we smile outside, the inside will smile as well." Monk looked towards the Cetiya. His expression still showed the initial joy of seeing the place for the first time. As though he could hear Charles's thoughts, Monk turned to him and said, "This Cetiya is the vision of our Master Abbot. Why is it shaped this way? Because as you walk around it, the shape will look the same from all directions. And the architecture of the dome shape provides the most structural stability. He gave this vision to an architect to design and build thirty years ago. Built with one million Buddha images sitting on the surface and within the dome, this Cetiya has helped many people fulfill their wishes."

Charles said, "This place is so awe-inspiring. Seeing it reminds me of the sculptures of the four US presidents at Mount Rushmore National Park, the Stonehenge of

England, or the Pyramids of Egypt. It's hard to forget these images."

Monk reflected on how Charles connected the Cetiya with monuments from some of the Wonders of the World. The Dhammakaya Foundation created this place to remind people to focus their minds on a round object during meditation. The mind's cognitive process needed tangible objects to cling on to and associate meanings with. Monk waited patiently without the feeling of pressure to strike up any small talk. A monk's mind is trained to be present by constantly connecting and centring his mind to the abdominal area of the body, which is also referred to as the seventh base of the mind.

Charles felt uncomfortable with the silence and needed to fill the space with conversation. He wanted to make the best use of the time and not 'waste' it by just sitting without talking. So he asked, "Excuse me for interrupting your thoughts, Monk Matt, but can I ask you some questions which have been bothering me for a long time?"

Monk smiled, "Of course."

Charles said, "I've seen how Toby has transformed from a troubled society dropout into someone so peaceful after he became a monk. I also noticed how monks around here look so serene. Can a person like me maintain a corporate career and achieve such peace, serenity, and happiness without becoming a monk?"

"Of course!" assured Monk Matt. "I will teach you three simple practices to achieve that. What else is bothering you?"

Charles went on to his next query. "You mentioned that the Law of Karma exists, and we need to do good deeds to accumulate more good merits. But what if that's not true, and the whole karma thing is just a... er... fraud... I mean, what if there is no such thing as karma? Wouldn't all my efforts go to waste? And who controls and keeps track of all our karma? God?"

Monk smiled again. "Great questions. Anymore?"

"This may be interrelated," said Charles, "but all I want to know is why I exist and what is my real purpose in life? Why am I here in this place? Am I destined to do something which I am fated to perform? I used to think that creating an impact on society and the economy was my contribution to the world. But I began to realise that it may only be a part of the whole plan for me. How do I know what my destiny is? That's all I want to know."

Monk then said, "You ask very good questions. But, what would knowing these answers do for you?"

THE RED OR BLUE PILL

Charles was taken aback by Monk's question. It was an excellent point as he questioned himself: *What would knowing about karma and my destiny do for me?* Charles had an IQ of 142, rated by Mensa to be among the top 1 per cent of the population of IQ demographics. He believed in science and data-driven logic. With an honours degree in Computer Science, he had planned his life based on practical rationalisation and structured thinking. Even his first child's sex was scientifically planned by meticulous steps, including eating the right food to create an alkaline environment in the female and drinking coffee to create the right environment to conceive a boy.

Charles stammered his reply, "Theresa and Antonio explained to me how they prioritised their lives after Prague. They shared a fantastic model to narrow down my most important Triple Gems, which are the three things that are most important to me till the day I die. I also realised that an average person spends one-third of his life sleeping, one-third of his life working, and one-third of his life doing other things for himself. However, Theresa made me realise that, for me, I spend more than two-thirds of my time sleeping and working, and have less than one-third of my time for myself and my family. So, I wanted to catch up to make sure that the next stage of my life is spent in a meaningful way. And since we don't know how much time we have in our lifetime, I wanted to start immediately. And if there is an afterlife, which I am not yet fully convinced of, I wanted to have a better life after this one. Does that make any sense, Monk? Because it does not fully make sense to me yet."

Monk nodded his head slowly as he listened to this executive revealing the vulnerable inner self under the facade of confidence. "Charles, this makes perfect sense to me. Your questions are similar to those many people have wondered but dared not ask for fear of the answers. People who refuse to seek answers to these simple yet powerful questions are living in denial or choose to be ignorant. Not knowing the law is not the excuse that will get you out of jail. For example, tourists visiting Singapore must know that bringing in or consuming drugs like marijuana carries a mandatory death sentence. It may be legal to smoke marijuana in cities like Amsterdam, but possession of the same stuff in Singapore will be against the law and subject to capital punishment. Claiming ignorance of that law will not get the person a lighter sentence. The Law of Karma is the same. Nobody taught us about this law in school, and scientific methods have not produced any empirical proof. It does not matter whether you believe it or not, it applies to every living creature on earth, heaven, or hell."

Charles nodded vigorously, agreeing about the strict laws in Singapore. Even the importation and selling of chewing gum is illegal in Singapore, where the government wanted to promote a 'clean and green' city.

Monk said, "Let's tackle the most difficult question on karma existence first. Once we address that, the other questions will be easier to deal with. Okay?"

Charles agreed.

Monk continued, "The Law of Karma was not created by Buddha, or the Hindus, or any God we know of. No one knows who created it. Buddha discovered it on his enlightenment journey through deep meditation. It is the foundational concept or law that explains Buddha's teaching of suffering.

If that is proven false, the entire teaching of Buddha would be discredited. In a similar way, the Christian faith would be threatened if the foundation theology of the religion, the resurrection of Jesus Christ, is proven false. Many have tried, but so far, the proof has not been conclusive.

"So, how does one prove the existence of karma? The Law of Karma is the law of action and its consequences. Karma means an intentional action and can be divided into two types: good karma or actions which bring about happiness; and bad karma or actions which bring about suffering. This cause and effect relationship constitutes the Law of Karma.

"Belief is a powerful part of our mind and can be a cognitive power or a spiritual power — the belief about this plane of existence and the next plane of existence, and about life in the hereafter; the belief that death is not annihilation, but that death leads to rebirth. These beliefs are key to how we will live our earthly life and how it will impact our next and future existences. One's beliefs determine if one will have a life of mostly happiness or suffering. The reason being that our beliefs influence our deeds and our deeds determine our lives. All beings are conditioned by their overall karma. We reap what we sow, as they say. If we do good deeds, we receive happiness as their consequence. If we commit bad deeds, we receive suffering as their consequence."

"But who is keeping track of all these?" asked Charles. "How do 'they' know every action being performed? Is there a god or a karma accountant up there responsible for tracking every single thought and action of every single being? That's massive!"

Monk was amused at the idea of a karma accountant, but he explained, "Maybe this analogy of the massive Internet might help you see how karma works. The Internet is connected to billions of devices and is changing every moment. Every choice you make on your computer or mobile device is recorded and stored, somewhere. The Internet and your device keeps a history of all the web locations you've visited, chats sessions you've had, documents you've created, read, or saved, passwords you've entered, shopping carts you've had, search keywords you've used, blogs you've posted, and even the results of your partially played games. Karma is similar to this. The karma system keeps a history of all the locations you've visited, conversations you've had and shared, secrets you've kept, deeds you've performed, friends you've helped or cheated, thoughts and even unfinished promises you've made.

"The search engines keep an index of every piece of information that has ever existed on the Internet, making it almost impossible to remove these memories of your past actions. In a limited way, with your devices, you can delete some history and data on your device, and some accounts on the Internet. For example, you can delete your Facebook account, remove all photos, clear your browser history, erase downloaded data, and clear your cache. The karma system, unfortunately, does not allow you to delete any actions you had done. Just like the Internet, your history of deeds, your thoughts and actions, are permanent and travel with you across all rebirths, just like your profile travels across all devices wherever you are connected online."

Charles exclaimed, "Wow! That analogy is amazing. No one single organisation controls the massive Internet. I can see the parallel between the Internet and the karma system and how the enormous amount of data and information that is gathered is just... there. But how do we know that the Law of Karma exists? There is no scientific evidence or proof of it."

Monk smiled and looked straight into Charles eyes. "Are you ready to take the blue pill or the red pill? You take the blue pill, you go back to the life you came from and believe whatever you choose to believe. You take the red pill, you go down the path of the truth, which may be harsh and difficult to accept. But you can never come back to the blissful world of ignorance, which could be more comfortable."

Charles knew exactly what Monk was referring to. In the science fiction movie, *The Matrix*, a person who swallows the red pill would become aware of the Matrix, which is a virtual reality world where humans are essentially program codes, controlled by larger computer programs and system codes. Someone who takes the blue pill would continue living in ignorance, thinking that the world of material bliss is the reality he chooses to believe in.

"The red pill!" said Charles immediately.

"Okay," said Monk. "Here is a fact. When we were in school, we learnt that there were nine planets in our solar system. But in 2006, this was disputed and Pluto was no longer a planet. It was reclassified as an exoplanet. So, we were wrong for seventy-six years since the discovery of Pluto in 1930. Here is another fact. For years, nutritionists had recommended whole wheat foods as the healthy carbohydrate. Other forms of carbs were less healthy. Meat and fats were worse than bad. A recent argument has surfaced to say that wheat contains gluten and it is the cause of coeliac disease, which is an inflammatory reaction to gluten that could lead to cancer. Some studies have also claimed that an all-protein diet with meat and fat, chunky unhealthy animal fats, could actually contribute to cholesterol reduction and also weight loss. So, who do we believe and what can we believe these days?"

Charles smiled knowing that he had switched his diets from carbs to no-carbs, to veg-only, to meat-only, before finally settling on 'anything in moderation'.

"The proof of karma can be tested by two methods," said Monk. "One method is to wait till you die to know if karma exists or not. The second way is to believe it wholeheartedly and experience it for yourself. If you believe in karma and lead a life doing good deeds, you will feel good, experience happiness and joy from thinking and doing these good deeds. In fact, you would even attribute all your good fortune, good luck, and success to you doing these good deeds. Some psychologists call these belief-bias, or self-fulfilling prophecy. But the caveat is that you have to believe it wholeheartedly for it to work.

"There are four possible scenarios of believing in karma. The first scenario is this. You believed in karma and it guided you to perform lots of good deeds. On the day you die, it is the ultimate end of existence and there is no rebirth and no karma. That meant that Buddha had misled all of mankind for 2,600 years. That's kind of like believing that wheat was good for you only to find out that it wasn't. What would happen next? Nothing! You've already enjoyed a happy and lucky life thinking that karma existed. Your belief had cultivated your mind to influence your deeds and delivered happy experiences.

"The second scenario. You believed in karma and it guided you to perform good deeds. On the day you die, you are relieved to know that the Law of Karma exists and that all your good deeds have helped you accumulate a bounty of good merits in your 'merit investment account'. It will secure you a better rebirth destination, perhaps as a healthy and wealthy human with wisdom or a celestial being without the burden of human sufferings.

"In the third scenario, you did not believe in the Law of Karma so led your life guided by your own judgement of right or wrong and moral or immoral. When you die, you are right and karma does not exist, so you do not suffer the retribution of some of your bad karmic actions. No loss, no gain, no consequences for your bad deeds. Poof!... and it is all over.

"Similarly, in the fourth scenario, you did not believe in the Law of Karma. Thus. you led your life according to your own judgement of right or wrong and moral or immoral. When you die, you realise that the Law of Karma does exist, and that your final rebirth destination will be determined by the merit and demerit points you have accumulated. You may not have accumulated sufficient good merits to be reborn as a human being or to ascend to a higher realm and be a celestial being. You may have to go through many cycles of rebirths as animals or stay in a fiery hell to clear your bad karma."

Charles asked, "Does that mean that a person who believes in Karma will always get good results? Will always be lucky and successful?"

"Not always," replied Monk Matt, "because some of the karmic results were brought forward from previous lifetimes, while some karma are the results from this lifetime of deeds. But a person who believes in karma would understand that some negative outcomes are the result of previous karma, which they could not control. Hence, they accept that once they serve or suffer through these negative effects, the bad karma will disappear. On the other hand, when they perform more good deeds, which they can control, they start accumulating good merits which brings success and 'luck' in this lifetime and beyond this lifetime."

"How does one's bad karma action get to be cleared completely?" asked Charles.

Monk explained, "Karma actions could be interlinked with so many causes and effects that it may not be easily cleared by a single action. So, you need to be careful when committing bad deeds because there are many ripple effects. Similarly, doing good deeds also has ripple effects of positive merits.

"For example, your neighbour has a dog that terrorises your kids and barks all day and night at everyone. One day, you intentionally drop some meat spiked with cyanide at the edge of your garden. Your neighbour's dog eats the meat and dies. This event leads to the depression of your neighbour's eighteen-year-old daughter. This event occurs a week before the daughter's crucial biology exam which is a key subject to her gaining admission into medical school. As a result, she never becomes a physician, but instead becomes a mechanical engineer. This event also results in your acrimonious relationship with your neighbour, whose signature would later be required to approve the sale of the joint land behind your houses, where a childcare centre for the neighbourhood was to be built. So you see, clearing a karmic action is not as simple as serving a sentence and being cleared of the offence. The best solution is not to commit bad karma. The thinking of bad thoughts does not create a karma effect, but a bad thought is likely to be a prequel to a bad action later, which has karmic effect."

Charles recognised this style of argument as Theoretical Rationality which involves using abstract concepts or theoretical models to arrive at logical conclusions. It is different from Practical Rationality where conclusions are substantiated by facts and data-driven analysis. He recalled a final-year course in Computer Science on Game Theory where he learnt about Pascal's Wager Theory. In the mid-1600s, physicist Blaise Pascal had determined that if a person wagered or believed that there was a God and that person is correct, then he gains an infinite amount of benefit. This benefit could be being able to live an eternal afterlife in heaven or being rewarded for believing in God for his entire life. Pascal also reasoned that if one was to believe in God, and God did not exist, then there is nothing to lose out on. The conclusion, as Pascal saw it, is that the potential benefits of believing in God's existence was so immense that given the choice between believing in God and not, believing is the better option every time.

"Okay," said Charles, "I think I can go along with accepting the belief in the Law of Karma. More to gain than lose. Then, how do I know my purpose and my destiny?"

Monk said, "You are not destined to be anything by anyone except your own karmic intentions and actions. There are some who believe that our life is predestined or fated, and there is a big heavenly book that has already written your destiny. The beauty of the Law of Karma is that we are accountable for all our results. Nothing is written and there is no powerful being who will judge you. The karma system judges you based on your own volition of decisions and actions. You reap what you sow.

"Your purpose and destiny are decided by you. You set your goals and decide what your life's purpose is, then you will know what path to take. Our Master, the Abbot, reminds us to make a daily resolution that includes the three Life wishes: Health, Wealth, and Wisdom. If you are very healthy but poor, you might live a long life in poverty. If you have wealth but weak health, you may spend a fortune healing your body. If you have wisdom but are not very wealthy or healthy, you may be a sickly professor, who is smart but unable to teach and hence cannot earn a living easily. Thus the ideal life is one that has the strength of good health, the richness of wealth, and the clarity of good wisdom. So, what is your purpose in life? It should at least include health, wealth, and wisdom. It's as simple as that!"

Charles joked, "How do I get all three? Is there another magic pill?"

Monk laughed. "No magic pill for this one. This one needs effort and commitment. Fortunately, there are some prescriptive actions you could take. Follow the three simple principles of living and you will achieve your destiny.

Firstly, if we want to have a healthy body, we need to observe strictly the 5 Precepts of being right. Secondly, if we want to have a wealthy life, we need to be generous and charitable. Thirdly, if we want wisdom, you can get it from practising meditation daily."

"This is an interesting prescription for creating your own destiny," said Charles. "I like it. These are very structured approaches. Could you tell me what the 5 Precepts are?"

Monk nodded, "The 5 Precepts are:

1. Do not take the lives of living beings.
2. Do not take what is not given.
3. Do not engage in sexual misconduct.
4. Do not lie or speak falsehoods.
5. Do not take intoxicants like drugs or alcohol."

Charles asked, "What constitutes sexual misconduct?"

Monk replied, "If you are married, do not have extramartial affairs. Do not cheat on your wife. If you are single, do not have sexual relationships with married people. Of course, there are other variations to this depending on the social norms, laws, and culture these days. But essentially, if you avoid these few misconducts that I mentioned, you are on a good starting block to observe Precept 3."

"If I drink only a sip of whisky a day, without being intoxicated, would that violate Precept 5?" asked Charles.

Monk explained, "Drugs and alcohol cause the mind to be 'unmindful', if there is such a word. Your conscious mind may not feel the intoxication of the alcohol, but it has already affected your biological function, whether you agree or not. The act of consuming alcohol is in itself violating Precept 5, not the quantity of that is consumed. A person may not walk wobbly or speak incoherently by drinking one glass of alcohol, but the alcohol already has affected his body and mental capacity. So yes, it would violate Precept 5."

Charles sighed. He had tried to 'flex' the precept to include his personal love for whisky, but Monk Matt did not cut him any slack. He realised that the human mind can be very sly and clever when it wanted the best of everything yet did not want to be restricted or change its old ways. Perhaps this would be the beginning of change. But throwing away his expensive whisky collection was a painful thought.

CAN I BE SUCCESSFUL BUT NOT BE A MONK?

Charles combed his fingers through his thick grey hair. "Looks like these laws and precepts overlap with some of the Bible's Ten Commandments. Thou shalt not kill; Thou shalt not steal; Thou shalt not commit adultery; Thou shalt not bear false witness against thy neighbour; Thou shalt not covet thy neighbour's wife. If I follow these 5 Precepts, does that mean I am closer to being as pure as a monk already?"

"Not yet," Monk chuckled. "A monk has 227 Precepts. You have a long way to go. But the 5 Precepts will be a very good start to lead a wholesome life."

Charles and Monk shared a light-hearted laugh. Just then, a volunteer arrived to offer some tea and biscuits. They both sipped hot tea while Charles bit into the ginger snaps. Charles noted that Monk did not eat the biscuits. Monk noticed the enquiring look on Charles's face and explained "Not eating meals after midday is the 6th Precept. Some laypeople observe more than the 5 Precepts. The reason for not eating after lunch is to keep the body devoid of processing food so that the mind can focus on meditation. It also helps with detoxifying the body daily through the fasting process. The only allowable intakes are water, some juices including honey, sugar cane, tamarind, tea, and orange after lunch."

Charles smiled, "I need that fasting diet. Can I swap the 6th Precept with the 5th? I think it's easier for me to fast than abstain from alcohol."

Monk shook his head as they both laughed heartily.

Charles sipped his Earl Grey tea, enjoying its fragrance. He then asked, "So Monk Matt, you were an aeronautics engineer before you became a monk. Do you think a person can attain happiness and success in a professional career but not pursue the life of a monk? Or can a person's ultimate happiness only be attained through monkhood?"

Monk smiled as he replied, "Any layperson can achieve success and happiness without being a monk. When a person observes the 5 Precepts and make a daily resolution to achieve good health, wealth, and wisdom, then align their life activities to these, they will achieve happiness. Monks need to set their life's goals as well. They have exactly the same destination, that is ultimate happiness in Nirvana. Both layperson and monk can achieve their life's goals, but do you know what the key difference is between a monk's life and a layperson's life?"

Charles thought aloud, "Hmm... the robe? Or the shaved head? Or the chanting? Superpowers from meditation?"

"It's the Precepts," said Monk Matt. "Monks are human too. They have a mother, a father, and friends. They have desires and a mind that thinks as wildly as any layperson. Just because Toby has donned the orange robe does not change who he is. The main difference is the 227 Precepts that monks observe without fail. These precepts guide their behaviour and give them the purity of thoughts, intentions, and actions. When you observe the 5 Precepts, you will realise that you will have purer thoughts, intentions, and actions. And when you use the karma system to guide your life, your path to happiness will be redefined, not by material excessiveness, but by intrinsic inner happiness."

"So technically," said Charles, "a layperson can also achieve enlightenment without having to be ordained as a monk, right?"

"Correct!" beamed Monk. "Except that, a monk can get there faster because the 227 Precepts trains his mind to be purer and clearer, and his simpler life does not have as many distractions, which is equivalent to stirring up the sediment at the bottom of the glass."

"Phew!" exclaimed Charles in relief. "It's a relief to know that I can still achieve enlightenment without having to be a monk. So I just set my life goals to focus on health, wealth, and wisdom by observing the Precepts, performing charitable acts, and meditating every day. Believe in the Law of Karma to guide my intentional actions. Do good, think good, and be joyful of other's success. Be compassionate and share loving kindness generously. Did I get all of it?"

Monk smiled. "If you can do what you just mentioned, that is better than most of the people in this world today."

Charles pushed on excitedly, "Since the ultimate happiness is Nirvana, does one automatically attain Nirvana after enlightenment?"

Monk remarked cautiously, "There are four stages of progress along the path of enlightenment before Nirvana. The first three stages are available to both laypeople and monks alike. The final stage of Arahatship requires one to lead a monastic life. Attaining the first stage of enlightenment, called Stream-Entrant or sotāpanna, could take aeons of lifetimes of purification."

Monk sensing a sudden disappointment in Charles, added encouragingly, "Would you like a special tip to get you a turbo boost for your journey to enlightenment and eventually Nirvana?"

"Yes! I'd love to have a FastPass!" exclaimed Charles.

"FastPass?" queried Monk.

Charles smiled. "A FastPass is a special ticket you get when you visit the Disney amusement parks in various parts of the world. With it, you can jump to the front of the normal queue and shorten the wait time for certain rides. It is especially useful for popular rides where the queue can take an hour or more. Other parks have it too, but it's known by different names."

"FastPass," said Monk thoughtfully, "I like that concept. Yes, there is a FastPass to Nirvana too. Like Toby, a layperson can be ordained to be a short-term monk for a minimum of thirty days. They can then return to lay life after this period. Short-term ordination has the benefit of allowing a person to be fully immersed in leading the life of a monk, with its 227 Precepts for thirty days. He is literally driving on the highway towards Nirvana. After the thirty days, he exits the highway, and returns to his normal layperson's life. Some people do a thirty-day ordination every three years just to get that FastPass to speed up their journey."

Charles's eyes widened. "Wow! That's a great concept. But I can't even take a week off from work. Thirty days is a big commitment."

Monk agreed. "Yes, it is a big commitment. Moreover, you would need your wife's and parents' approval so that you don't leave them in distress when you go away on your FastPass ride. IDOP runs ordination programmes yearly. So whenever you are ready, just let me know."

"That's really good to know," smiled Charles. "I will take a rain check on that offer."

Monk's eyebrows came together slightly, "Rain check?"

Charles chuckled. "Never mind! Sorry, I am using too many American terms here. You teach me more of the Pāli language; I promise to teach you American jargon some day."

Monk smiled. "Are all your questions answered?"

"Yes, more than I expected," said Charles. "I know how to plot my path to retirement and set my goal towards happiness. And I know I have a FastPass to use when I need to."

"Remember, we do not know how much time we have in this life," Monk cautioned. "So every day we wake up is an event to rejoice. Do not take it for granted."

Charles nodded. "That is a good reminder, which also means that I need to take action immediately, because we are running out of time. Thank you, Matt... er... Monk Matt. Now I know the meaning of that meeting at Kampa Park. Something made me walk from my bench to the tree where you were sitting that day. It was not by accident. It was probably my good karma to have the opportunity to meet Monk Matt at the height of my career when I can still plan ahead. Thank you!"

"May you achieve your happiness and have the wisdom to act on the plans," Monk wished Charles. "May your mind be clear and pure to perform charity and observe the precepst to lead a long healthy life of happiness and wealth."

Charles replied, "Thanks Matt… err… sorry, I meant Monk Matt."

Monk smiled and replied, "Sadhu."

Taking a cue from Monk, Charles responded with clasped palms, "Sadhu!"

THE EXIT

Two days before the end of the fiscal year

For most businesses, the end of the financial year was the most pressurising period for everyone. There was always the mad rush and race against the clock to get more sales and utilise the budget expenditure. Salespersons would be trying to lock in their final sales in order to get them counted for their year-end bonuses and commissions. Accounting departments would be fighting to prevent the business departments from approving any more expenditure so that they could finalise the numbers and close their financial books.

The Leadership Strategic Retreat weekend in Bangkok six months ago in January had paid off. Charles's Scorecard Dashboard on his computer showed that his Key Performance Indicators — or KPIs, as they are more commonly known — were all green. This meant that the measurements were above target. Red meant measurements were below target and orange indicators meant there was a risk of missing the target.

At the retreat in Bangkok, Charles had led his team through an intense weekend of planning, motivation, and inspiration. He used the Life's Inventory exercise, which Theresa had documented, to guide the team to develop their personal top three priorities, which he called the Triple Gems. The Triple Gems were the three Life Inventory items that a person would value most till the last day of his life. By filtering through all the 'Want', 'Nice-to-have', and 'Must-have' items, a person going through the Life Inventory exercise would consciously select only the top three — his personal Gems — that meant the most to him.

Charles said to the team, "What you wrote down are your top three priorities. These must be the same priorities that you will keep doing till your last breath. Your Triple Gems will guide you to See, Think, Say, and Act in a certain way that will lead you to the end result. So what you write will be, so to speak, your moral compass that will guide you on your own path.

"The only thing you can bring with you to your next existence is your mind and your Karma Bucket. Your Karma Bucket has the entire history and memories of all your past deeds, both good and bad. So choose wisely what you commit to do every day. Your bad habits need to change to good habits. Your good actions need to be repeated until they became a habit which are second nature to you." Charles then shared his personal Triple Gems with the team and encouraged everyone to share theirs openly. On Charles's list was:

1. Health: to exercise daily; maintain a monks-diet routine five times a week (i.e. two meals daily, no dinner)
2. Wealth: have a financial plan; work hard and give away 50 per cent of income; to live fully and to give fully
3. Wisdom: meditate daily for a clear and bright mind

That exercise was very emotional. and it bonded his leadership team members deeply at their hearts. This was one of the main reasons that his team was able to put personal interests aside to collaborate for a team win. At first his team was confused by Charles's Triple Gems because they did not include any business goals and priorities. They were worried that their boss has gone soft and was losing it with all his monk talk. Then Charles explained that the purpose of the exercise was to focus an individual's priorities to the three most important assets to himself, regardless of any external expectations, and that when a person's Gems were aligned to the team members', the team would perform at an extraordinary level. The team then started to realise that this was not just career planning; it was life planning.

Charles introduced The Results Pathway to the team. They all loved the framework. It was so simple to understand and it made them aware of all the Blame Actions that most people indulge in whenever they hit a problem. They acknowledged that Blame Actions were not useful, yet people spent so much time on it.

The four Right Action steps of See Right, Think Right, Say Right, and Act Right helped the team work collaboratively towards solving their problems. They recognised that in order to practise the Right Action steps, they needed to change their Beliefs and Attitudes.

This was where the Triple Gems came in. Each person's Triple Gems became their new Beliefs. This allowed them to match their personal priorities to their personal belief system. These Beliefs would, in turn, influence their Attitudes and Intentions towards the Right Actions. Subsequently, the team built a set of action plans based on The Result Pathway framework. They identified common Team Beliefs and Team Attitudes and aligned them to the Team Results.

Charles told them, "We have to start taking all the small actions and implement the Inch by Inch strategy. Don't be greedy. Everyone needs to find an inch of an advantage in their positions and play as a team. Together these inches will add up to yards. We are guided by our Intentions, Attitudes, and Beliefs. If we don't have the right attitudes, and belief in the success of the team, we won't execute on the action plans well."

The company's financial year starts on 1 July and ends twelve months after. So 30 June is the last day of the financial year. By 1 July, everything (sales, budgets, goals, commitments) resets back to zero, and a new set of sales targets begin again for another twelve months. With all his KPIs showing green on the Scorecard Dashboard, Charles wanted to celebrate and recognise the hard work of his team. He sat back at his desk, overlooking the Marina Bay Sands, thinking: *This has been a tough six months. We made it through! The business recovery is fantastic. And the models we created helped everyone operate as ONE TEAM. It feels so good. This is what happiness is!*

Charles smiled and breathed deeply. The past twelve months had changed his way of thinking and living. The meeting at Prague started everything. He recalled that Monk Matt had mentioned, several times, that nothing happens by accident. Charles set his financial goals, and was clear that this year's bonus would bring him over the top of his personal assets. He then diligently sent out donations to the charities and orphanages supported by the company's social responsibility efforts. Personally, Charles had been donating some funds to support Monk Matt's effort to improve the IDOP training facilities. And he had been addicted to meditation. He and Amy had just completed a private sixteen-week 'Introduction to Meditation' programme by a yoga master at their home.

Charles buzzed Sandra, his Business Manager, and asked that she organise an All-Hands meeting for Friday, the last day of the financial year. They needed to cater some food and get a big cake with the words '$500M' written across to celebrate grossing more than $500 million in sales.

"And a few crates of beer and some wine, boss?" she asked.

Charles shook his head. "No alcohol this time."

Sandra raised her eyebrows. "Really? No alcohol at a team party? That's not normal, boss. You sure?"

Charles wanted to skip alcohol because he was trying to observe the 5th Precept, but then he thought that his life's goals may not be everyone's personal life's goals. His observance of the 5 Precepts was a personal choice, and he should not impose that on others. He wished that the younger employees could hear Monk Matt's discourse on Karma and the Life Goal. He thought: *Maybe next time, at the next retreat, I will invite Monk to speak.*

"Okay Sandra, go ahead with the alcohol. Let the spirit flow!" said Charles.

Sandra grinned, "Yeah! That's the boss I am used to!"

He looked at a crumpled sheet from his note pad. It was stuck on the glass window in an obscure corner which only Charles could see from his seat behind his computer monitor. All items were checked as 'Done' except for item number 6.

6. To quit my corporate job. Retire from M-Reality by 31 Dec, three years from today

Charles thought: *Hey I can wait two more years then*

retire or I could retire now while I am at the top of my game. I could serve six more months as transitional CEO and help identify my successor. During that period, I can also take some courses to get myself ready for a new Executive Coaching business. And also work on writing my book.

He did not want to make a rash decision to quit, as he had two more years to plan it right. But he wanted to set the wheel in motion for his retirement, so he started to write his resignation letter, undated, and have it ready at anytime. *No excuses this time,* he thought.

Date: _____

Dear Ted,

I'd like to inform you that I would like to resign from the company. I propose that my last day with M-Reality to be around 1 August after the fiscal year ends. I will dedicate six months to get a transition plan through the second half of the fiscal year. I have a list of suitable successors and will work with you to develop them to ensure a smooth transition. I look forward to your support of my decision.

I am planning to take a year off work to restart my life and to reprioritise things around me. Life is about living, loving, and giving. By the next World Wide Sales Meeting (WWSM) in August, we should have identified my successor and we can announce that decision then.

I was hoping that the WWSM could be held in Prague again as I love that city. But I hear that the city has sold out all their Bohemian crystals after we bought everything :-). By the way, if you want a spiritual leader Keynote Speaker, I know of a really good Monk, who is pursuing a PhD in World Peace Studies. He could teach us about how to meditate, enabling us to balance Success and Happiness.

As my final contribution to the company, I would like to take the leadership team through a model to build high performance teams. That will be the foundation of my new coaching and consulting practice, The Results Pathway methodology.

Cheers

Charles Takashi Wantanabe

10

THREE YEARS LATER

The best things in life are free.
The second best things are very, very expensive.
- Coco Chanel -

TWILIGHT SAIL

Charles stood at the helm of his ten-metre sail boat shouting, "Tacking! Tacking! Tacking! Now!". 'Tacking' is a sailing term for a manoeuvre where the boat is turned into the direction of the oncoming wind.

Toby shouted, "Go around from the outside! The wind is cleaner there!"

Charles and his crew were in a Twilight Race around Singapore's Ubin Island. They were sailing on the Beneteau First 35.5, a 1980 French-made racing sail boat, which Charles had named *Sama-Arahang*, meaning "clear and virtuous". They are inching from third placing to overtake *Sweet Phoenix* at the final turn of buoy marker #7 before sailing downwind back to the finishing line.

Antonio was frantically winching in the line, using a fast rotary motion, like the crew at an America's Cup yacht race. He needed to pull in the ropes of the main sail fast, in order to catch the wind and not lose momentum. Then the sail had to be kept taut at the perfect sailing angle. Toby was hanging precariously over the side rail, intensely looking out for any change of direction of the wind.

Once they made that tack and the sail was set in the right direction, everyone relaxed. They had just made an aggressive tactical move to take the outer line in order to catch a stronger wind and overtake their sailing friends on the *Sweet Phoenix*. Now they were in second position, about two boat lengths from *Passion*, the boat in the first position ahead of them. Charles was very happy to be in second position. He told the crew, "It's more relaxing being in second position. Nobody remembers who comes in second, but that's the way I like it. We are competing to win, but it's too tense to be in the first position. Being in the front pack is good enough for me. Second place is the perfect pace to balance fun, relaxation, and be happy."

Theresa emerged from the cabin with drinks for everyone. "Champagne everyone? To the happiest crew to come in second place!"

Everyone laughed and toasted to a pleasant sunset sail back to the Changi Sailing Club.

EPILOGUE

THE CEO, CHARLES TAKASHI WATANABE

- Living in Osaka, Japan
- Retired from the corporate world
- Built a niche consulting practice
- Goes for meditation retreats thirty days in a year

His Journey

It took Charles twenty months to finalise the detailed plans of the exit from his corporate career. It was a very tough decision to leave the corporate world after dedicating twenty-five years of his life to it. Three years after the meeting at Kampa Park, Charles retired from the corporate world. How did he make that decision?

Charles recalled the evening he told Amy and both his children about his decision to leave the corporate life behind. He started by telling them a story. "In the past few months, I met three celestial angels — the Monk, an Entrepreneur, and a Tourist.

"The Monk taught me that Happiness is not about having more, but about having less. A simple life is not about wealth versus poverty, or sophistication versus simplicity. **A simple life** is about adopting a daily habit to detach yourself from the desires of material things, appreciate the present, and accumulate more merits by doing good wholesome deeds. Most importantly, he taught me that **Mindfulness** is not a task. Mindfulness is a state of mind, of being aware that things are not permanent and that we need to let go of our fixed expectations. The initiation of a single thought begins the process of mindfulness. A mindful thought will lead to mindful views, mindful speech, mindful actions, and mindful results.

"The second angel was a work-obsessed, trailblazing, and goal-oriented Entrepreneur. He was a mirror that reflected many images of my own behaviours. The Entrepreneur taught me about **Greed and Anger**. The practice of meditation helps release the mind from being stuck with one's own judgement and beliefs. When the mind exercises Compassion, we step into another person's world and see things with their eyes. In order to gain an understanding of others, we must first offer compassion. Most people attempt to understand others by intellectual comprehension — that usually leads to the judgement of others and hinders compassion. When we give compassion first, we begin to gain a real understanding of others' plights and points of view. When we begin to look for the gemstones in the mud, we begin our self-discovery to find inner fulfilment in every experience in this lifetime.

"The third angel was a severely depressed alcoholic Tourist. He taught me by showing me his amazing recovery from the **delusion** in his life, by giving up everything and letting go of all attachments. He restarted himself and taught me that the more I take control of my life, the less control I have. By letting go of the mental and cognitive control of how I define and architect my life, I was able to redefine contentment and happiness in my life. He taught me that I needed to empty my cup, before I could fill it up again."

After Charles quit his corporate job, he took six months to recharge his batteries by attending conferences, obtaining certification as a professional coach, and reading lots of books on organisational development. Eventually, he started a consulting firm to organise workshops and coach.

242 A CEO, AN ENTREPRENEUR, A TOURIST, AND THE MONK

Charles moved back to Osaka with the family so he could visit his mother weekly. His two children transferred to the International School there. His mother was very happy to be able to see more of her grandchildren.

Charles's Triple Gems

1. Health: to exercise daily; maintain a monk's diet routine five times a week (i.e. two meals daily, no dinner)
2. Wealth: have a financial plan; work hard and give away 50 per cent of income; to live fully and to give fully
3. Wisdom: meditate daily for a clear and bright mind

Just when you think you control the Mind,
it has already controlled you.
Let go of everything, and the Mind will come back to you.
- Charles Takashi Watanabe, the CEO -

* * *

THE ENTREPRENEUR, ANTONIO ANGER

- Married Theresa
- Sold half his businesses
- Funds start-ups
- Conducts meditation workshops

THERESA VITOVA

- Married Antonio
- Travelled round the world
- Teaches the 'Triple Gems to Happiness'
- Lives in Prague

Their Journey

A year after they met, Antonio and Theresa were married. They held their wedding in Prague, marking the beginning of their relationship. Their honeymoon was celebrated by travelling and exploring the world for twelve months. During their travels, Antonio focused on advancing his meditation technique while Theresa focused on developing the Life Inventory Framework. She called it the Triple Gems to Happiness. At the end of their travels, Theresa launched her workshop in Prague, targeting newly-weds.

Prague is a destination for newly-weds and honeymooners and couples looking to re-invigorate their fatigued relationships. Antonio was able to tie up with tour companies and wedding planners to conduct these workshops and seminars for couples so that they set their life's priorities right from the start. This concept appealed to couples as the life inventory exercise was the perfect foundation to achieve their happy-ever-afters. Wedding tour companies loved this package as it differentiated them from the regular tours. And since Theresa could speak multiple languages, her workshop became an instant success.

Antonio and Theresa invested many months during their travels to learn advanced meditation practices from several masters around the world. Sometimes Antonio would spend several weeks in a forest learning about breathing techniques from one master. They had learned masters who taught visualisation, yoga techniques, and even those who focused on pains. Eventually, Antonio developed simple and easy-to-follow instructions to learn meditation that would fit into the busy lives of laypeople. Most people do not have patience and time to hone their skills and get deep into meditation. Many of the masters taught meditation using traditional hardcore learning methods which required physical endurance and pushed the mental tolerance to the limits.

Antonio managed to sell off all of his restaurant and franchise businesses. Some of these were sold to the franchisee owner-operators, others were sold to corporate investors. Antonio continued to be the silent investor for the few start-up businesses he had under his belt, but he gave 49 per cent of his share to the pioneer team members of these start-ups. He became a business coach to these entrepreneurs, which is what he wanted to do all along.

Antonio reflected on his own Life Inventories' Triple Gems, which he had developed with Theresa in Prague three years ago. It had guided him to balance success and happiness.

As for Theresa, her life had finally come together with a purpose and meaning. Her aspiration to travel and see the world was now a reality. Antonio was always so loving and supportive of her work. She never knew the old version of Antonio, but he constantly reminded her that she was an 'Angel' sent to help him change his life. Theresa quietly believed that the accidental encounter in Kampa Park was the fruit of her good Karma. Meeting a good man and being able to work with him to create an impact on the world is what made her happy. Her workshops created a better start for newly-wed couples and she got to stay in Prague. *What more could I wish for?* she thought to herself. Perhaps one more…

Theresa tested positive — she was pregnant, finally! She and Antonio had been trying for a child for a year, unsuccessfully. Perhaps all the stress of the wedding and travelling had made it difficult to conceive. Or perhaps, they were finally receiving the fruits of their merits from their good deeds, generosity, and meditation She was excited to announce it to Antonio.

Antonio's Triple Gems
1. Giving: Spread Joy, Compassion, and Charity
2. Teacher: Coach and teach others, start-ups, entrepreneurs
3. Spiritual: Develop inner peace through meditation

Theresa's Triple Gems
1. Life partner: Antonio
2. Travel the world
3. Be a good mother

To Receive is a Gift; To Give is a Privilege.
- Antonio Anger, the Entrepreneur -

* * *

THE TOURIST, TOBY TANNER

- Completed two years as a monk
- Spent one year in Korea as a K-pop dance instructor
- Back in Malaysia with Dad

His Journey

Toby stood at the door staring at the digital lock numeric pad. For 5 minutes, he was unable to recall the code that unlocked the door to his dad's dance studio. Typically, he would be frustrated and punching the wall in anger. But Toby just sighed in relief that the code was one of those events from his past that he had left behind.

It was 7.20 a.m., and Toby had just arrived from the airport having returned from Seoul, South Korea. It had been almost three years since Toby left home to be a monk. A year ago, he disrobed from monkhood and return to a layperson's life. He started a career in Korea as a recruiter and trainer of K-pop dancers. Within those twelve months, 100 per cent of his recruits made it into major K-pop groups. It was not an easy task as K-pop in Korea was very competitive. What made his teams successful was one unique secret 'move' that all other K-pop groups did not possess — the ability to manage their lives and stress through daily meditation. Toby's daily routine required everyone to meditate three times a day. Every day, they would meditate at 10 a.m., 2 p.m., and 5 p.m. Whatever they were doing during the day, everyone must stop at these three times to meditate for 20 minutes.

His boss was very impressed with Toby's techniques of teaching dance, integrated with spiritual values and meditation. They made him an offer to operate a K-pop recruitment company from Malaysia, looking for fresh talent overseas and expand K-pop outside of Korea.

Returning to Malaysia, Toby was very confident that he could now confront his old life and integrate his learning from the monastery into his life. His two years as a monk had allowed him to take control of his mind, learn deeply about himself, and build self-awareness and self-confidence. He could control his desires and manage the emotions of anger and hatred, and avoid the blame game through daily meditation. Toby embraced the 5 Precepts to lead his life.

1. No killing of living beings
2. No stealing
3. No sexual misconduct
4. No false speech (e.g. lying)
5. No consumption of intoxicants

Toby held their offer letter in his hands and thought: *Maybe I could convince Dad to modernise his dance studio and incorporate K-pop dance. Hmm, that would be interesting.*

But that was not his priority for today. Today, he wanted to surprise everyone with his return, hence no one was expecting him that morning. Putting his backpack against the wall, under the door buzzer, Toby sat down cross-legged to meditate. Perhaps someone would come in early today to open the studio. He would like a shower and to see his dad and perhaps Jessy. While meditating, Toby reflected on his life as a monk and his short stint in Korea.

DING! The lift's door opened. Jessy and Toby's father walked out of the lift carrying a breakfast basket to start the early Breakfast Club dance class. The looks on their faces were priceless when they saw a bald-headed Toby sitting at the door.

Toby's Triple Gems
1. The 5 Precepts as the moral compass
2. Meditation for clarity of the mind
3. Live mindfully, away from delusion

Life is what you make it.
Value every moment you have.
Time is your most precious gift for anyone,
because it's a part of your life that can never be re-lived.
- Venerable Toby Tanvanamo (Toby's monastic name) -

* * *

THE MONK, MATT SOMCHAI

- Completed his PhD thesis in World Peace Studies
- Still a monk after thirteen years

His Journey

Monk Matt finally graduated with a Doctorate in Philosophy in World Peace Studies. His thesis was so well-written that his doctoral advisor and thesis mentor, Professor Thomson, decided to send it to his old friend, Olof Alexander, who was the head of the United Nations Peace Council or UNPC. Three months later, Monk Matt received a call from Professor Thomson telling him that Alexander's secretary from UNPC wanted to interview him about his thesis paper. They wanted to invite him to be the guest speaker at the UN Assembly Plenary Session for Peace.

Upon receiving this news, Monk Matt was at a loss at what to do. Never did he expect his work would take a global stage as big as this. He consulted with the Seniors at his temple and was instantly given permission to accept the invitation. Monk Matt brought eight senior monks, who specialised in advanced meditation, with him to the UN meeting. He delivered a speech that moved the entire assembly and together with the eight monks, they ran a two-hour workshop on 'Meditation for World Peace' to about three hundred attendees. It was so successful that the UNPC wanted him to create a Peace Initiative with a mandate to use meditation as the common medium of communication. They wanted to spread this initiative to fifty countries, reaching out to one million people in five years.

Alexander offered Monk Matt the job of Chief Executive for the Initiative. Monk Matt could operate in any country, but he had to be in Geneva every three months to update the Council. The project had the endorsement of the UNPC, but it had to be self-funded through fund-raising from private organisations.

The Seniors at the Monastic Council recognised the opportunity to accelerate and spread the message of World Peace through loving kindness and meditation. This had been the vision of the Dhammakaya Foundation organisation — World Peace Through Inner Peace. One senior monk who was a mentor to Monk Matt said to him, "The day you were ordained thirteen years ago, I knew this day would come. This has always been your mission and your Kamma. Make it happen. You have my blessing and support."

Monk Matt was excited about the new Initiative. However, a monk could not take on a secular job or work in a secular organisation. He was not prepared to disrobe from the monkhood to accept this job as the Chief Executive. His life's mission was to be a monk and he wanted to die as a monk. That was the promise he made to himself when he wished for his mother's recovery from her illness thirteen years ago.

During meditation, a vision came to him. He saw a peaceful place surrounded by thousands of trees on an endless green field. In the middle of this field was one tree that stood taller than the rest. It had extensive branches that spread its shade wide and roots that spread far from its base. Under the tree sat a monk surrounded by four persons. There was a man in a navy blue suit, a bearded man in a leather jacket, a young man with a head full of curly hair, and a young lady. They seemed to be engaged in an animated and lively conversation. That vision was very surreal. In an instant, he realised the meaning of the 'accidental' encounter at Kampa Park in Prague, more than three years ago. As he opened his eyes from meditation, Monk Matt had a serene smile on his face, because he had found the answer to his challenge.

Monk Matt sent a message to Theresa and requested that she contact Toby, Antonio, and Charles. He needed their help on a mission to save the world. With the help of Toby, who set up a video conference call, Monk explained the entire situation to the four of them. "And that is why Monk feels you might be able to help," he concluded.

Over the next week, Charles, Antonio, Toby, and Theresa brainstormed on possible solutions to help Monk Matt. This project required the experience and organisational skills of a CEO. It needed someone with an entrepreneurial spirit to be creative, with a trailblazing energy to drive this initiative fast and not be bogged down by any bureaucracy. Toby's computer wizardry and free-spirited nature made him the perfect digital brainchild for this project. Theresa's love for travel, together with her charisma, meant she was a natural to handle logistics and events management for the programme. Monk Matt would be the spiritual sponsor leader working in the background, as the liaison with the various representatives of different religious sects. Charles strategised the business and financial plan. Antonio added the go-to-market details of the marketing plans. Toby created the conceptual plans for the website and social media strategy. Theresa put them all together into a fifty-page presentation package. After getting Monk Matt's endorsement of the plans, they sent it off to the UNPC for approval.

Monk Matt's Triple Gems
1. The Lord Buddha as his Teacher
2. The Dharma as his knowledge
3. Sangha and Peace Agents as his community of Peace

When I am in peace, the world is in peace.
World peace begins with inner peace.
- Abbot of Wat Phra Dhammakaya, Luang Por Dhammajayo -

REFERENCES

Peace Revolution is a project initiated by the World Peace Initiative Foundation. It aims to bring peace through the practice of meditation and mindfulness. In order to do so, the project organises fellowships, retreats, mindfulness, and meditation workshops and other activities all over the world, engaging people who want to work on their self-development. As its unique asset, Peace Revolution offers a free 42-day self-development programme teaching the skills and techniques involved in the development of inner peace. It provides guided meditation videos and daily reflections to support personal development and the practice of mindfulness.

In 2010, Peace Revolution has spread to more than 236 countries and territories serving more than 109,070 individuals with the 42-day self-development programme.

Begin your journey of change today!

Peace In, Peace Out
www.peacerevolution.net

ACKNOWLEDGEMENTS

I'd like to acknowledge the following people who contributed to this book:

Thoo Yuet Yeng (Mum)
Ang Ai Boon, Kris (Glides Consulting, Singapore)
Jonathan Butt (Fall Guy Consulting, Seattle, USA)
Julianne Butt (Occidental College, California, USA)
Butt Lai Peng, Clara (Signarama Asia, Singapore)
Ching Aik Chuan (Right Engineering Pte Ltd, Singapore)
John Delano (Retired CEO, Vancouver)
Steve Feniger (55 Consulting Ltd, Hong Kong)
Richard Hong (Retired CEO, Singapore)
Agnija Kazusa (Peace Revolution Project)
Nick Keomahavong (Family Therapist, California, USA)
Henry Lee (Glides Consulting Partners, Singapore)
Low Huoi Seong (New Vision Media Sdn Bhd, Malaysia)
Mok Yuen Lok (Crowe Horwath International, Asia)
Venerable Narongchai Thanajayo (Dhammakaya Foundation)
Patricia Ng (Candid Creation Publishing LLP, Singapore)
Phoon Kok Hwa (Candid Creation Publishing LLP, Singapore)
Saw Ken Wye (Crimsonlogic Pte Ltd, Singapore)
Teh Lip Kim (Selangor Dredging Berhad, Malaysia)
Wong Mun Yin, Benson (Retired Entrepreneur, Singapore)
Rick Wong (The Five Abilities® LLC, USA)
Yong Yun Seong (Expedia Inc., Singapore)

ABOUT THE AUTHOR

 ALEX BUTT transformed himself from a multinational corporate executive into a successful Coach and Entrepreneur. Since 2010, he has coached and transformed many organisations and entrepreneurs.

Prior to this and at his peak, Alex was leading Microsoft's most profitable business, the OEM division, in the Asia Pacific. He started his career as a Systems Engineer at Honeywell and subsequently became a Support Manager at Hewlett-Packard before spending 17 'intense and defining' years at Microsoft.

Alex has a Mensa-level IQ and became a millionaire at the age of 35. At the height of his career, at the age of 49 and after 25 years in the corporate world, he gave up the suit to pursue the path of an entrepreneur. Though spiritually agnostic, on his 56th birthday, his consciousness compass guided his decision to be ordained as a Buddhist monk. This led him to reboot himself by spending 45 days in seclusion in the forests of Thailand.

Alex believes in pushing career plus physical and mental states to the limit of their potential. "It's not about being an extremist, rather about being alive, constantly striving and balancing the best of bodily health, material wealth, and the inner wisdom of the mind. Find your balance and you will discover happiness."

Calling All Professionals, Business Owners and Entrepreneurs, Speakers and Trainers, Coaches and Consultants, Property Agents and Financial Planners

So You Want To Be An Author

Developing Your Blueprint for Publishing Success

4 REASONS WHY YOU SHOULD BE A PUBLISHED AUTHOR

- Pump up your visibility and increase your presence in the market. With the expanded mindshare you enjoy, you are able to attract more prospects and partners knocking on your door.
- Establish authority in the market without the need to brag. Because book authors are viewed as experts in their field, the trust you gain helps you to convert prospects to better, higher paying clients quickly.
- Build your personal brand and boost your credibility without having to spend thousands of dollars to run expensive advertising or marketing campaigns.
- Spread your ideas to a wider audience even without your physical presence. A book is like a name card on steroids helping you to spread your message and promote you and your business while you are sleeping.

So You Want To Be An Author is a 2-day hands-on authorship workshop specifically tailored to help game changers like you who aspire to stay at the top of their game by becoming published authors of non-fiction books. In this workshop, you will be guided to develop your own personal blueprint for publishing success using our 6P Framework of Publishing™. This the exactly the same proven framework that over 300 of our authors have followed to take them from just having an idea in their mind to enjoying success today as published authors.

Plan > Pen > Prepare > Produce > Promote > Publicise

LEARNING OUTCOME

- How to identify a niche and develop the contents for a book
- How to nurture your book from idea to market
- What are the critical success factors that can make or break a book
- How to get others to pay for your book before it is even published
- What you must do to market your book to gain maximum exposure
- How to generate free publicity for you, your book and your business

REGISTER TODAY:
http://candidcreation.com/services/authorship-workshop

" Engaging, experienced, masterful in pedagogy, Kok Hwa delivered way beyond my expectations in this workshop: not only did I learn what I need to do to get my book published, but I got to advance my work on it significantly. I have gained clarity and positive energy to make it happen soon."

Jean-Francois Cousin, Global Executive Coach, GREATNESS Leadership Coaching, author of *Game Changers at the Circus*

Workshop facilitators

Phoon Kok Hwa is a Publisher at Candid Creation Publishing, where he has spent the last decade helping hundreds of aspiring authors to get their books written, published, distributed and marketed. Kok Hwa is a literary agent at heart, nurturing and extracting the potential book out of every aspiring author. Apart from his personal beliefs in author expression, he also believes in a pragmatic aspect to publishing a book–personal branding–often stating that nothing produces instant credibility faster than giving away a book as a calling card. Kok Hwa is also a certified as a Professional Action Learning Coach by the World Institute for Action Learning and also a recipient of the International Coaching Excellence Award 2015.

Andrew Chow is a passionate social media and public relations strategist, entrepreneur, speaker and author of *Social Media 247*, *Public Relations 247*, and *Personal Branding 247*. Based in Singapore, his insights into social media strategy, media management and entrepreneurship have made him a choice selection for workshops and public speaking engagements across Asia,through which he educates professionals on how to leverage social channels for business results. Andrew's career has seen him work with an array of clients including AXA Insurance, Abbot Medical Optics, Singtel and Sony Pictures.

ALUMNI HALL OF FAME

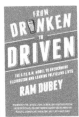

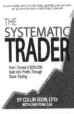

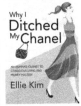

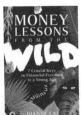

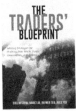

Order your copy today at http://candidcreation.com/bookshop/

CPSIA information can be obtained
at www.ICGtesting.com
Printed in the USA
LVHW041530151218
600594LV00005B/1746/P

9 789811 165085